take my hand

take my hand

KERRY FISHER AND PAT SOWA

Thread

Published by Thread in 2020

An imprint of Storyfire Ltd.
Carmelite House
50 Victoria Embankment
London EC4Y 0DZ

www.thread-books.com

ISBN: 978-1-83888-634-9
eBook ISBN: 978-1-83888-633-2

To my little warrior family, and everyone else battling away in the eye of a sudden storm. May these be our worst days.

Kerry Fisher

For Jan, Greg and Dom. I love you to Pluto and back a googolplex times.

Pat Sowa

A share of profits will go to the following charities:
Papyrus Prevention of Young Suicide and the Teenage Cancer Trust

Hello there,

Thank you for choosing to read our book. It reflects our personal experiences and we wrote it to provide some comfort and companionship. We wanted to reassure anyone who is going through difficult times, or helping someone who is, that they're not the only ones and that even if you can't see it, hope is always round the corner. It's absolutely not our intention to hurt anyone so we wanted to let you know that our life stories may well be close to your own and might elicit difficult memories or emotional pain. Please take care when reading and do not hesitate to reach out for help if you need support.

With love,
Kerry and Pat

CHAPTER ONE

Pat

A Cloudless Sky

June 2016

'Who's that?' asks Jan, watching me tap another message into the phone. I press send then place it carefully in my eyeline on the train table, face up so that I can see if anything comes through.

'Just checking in with Dom. I've finished now,' I say.

My husband, Jan, and I are on our way to celebrate the fiftieth birthday of my friend, Kerry, who I met at university back in 1984. It's been in the diary for ages and I've been looking forward to a break but now it's here I'm struggling to find my inner party animal. My energy is torn between time for Jan and me to let our hair down with Kerry and her husband, Steve, people who know us inside out, and being at home with an eagle eye on my son, Dom. He's sixteen, old enough to get married apparently, but I'm not ready to let him be in charge of the house so he's staying with a friend. Worry, my ever-present companion for the last couple of years, ebbs and flows as it mirrors Dom's own fragile state of mind. I resent it, resist it and try to rationalise it. But it will not go away.

I force myself into good-wife mode and focus on being with Jan. I remind myself that Dom is sensible underneath it all and I'll soon hear if anything goes wrong.

When we arrive at the party house in the woods, it is already filled with the voices of the other guests, spilling into the garden in the warm June sun. I get my happy hat on, and, with a deep breath, dive into the conversation. I'm slightly self-conscious that I'm the only one whose husband has been invited – Kerry deemed her celebration a girls' weekend but Jan is Kerry's closest male friend, and she declared, 'My party, my rules.' The house is full of Kerry's friends, an eclectic mix collected across the years, spanning childhood, school days, university and beyond. It's a bit like being at a wedding where the only connection is knowing the bride, so a huge grin breaks across my face as I hug Maria and Gel, good mates who were with us studying in Bath over thirty years ago. At last I reconnect with my younger, go-with-the-flow self, and it doesn't take long for the heady sense of escape from life's trials to warm me up. I relax into the chatter as we put on our walking boots and head out for a 'constitutional' on the South Downs.

As we get into our stride, the group spreads out and I listen intently to the stories of other mothers. Somehow the intimacy and anonymity of coming together like this has released the usual conventions and I hear about eating disorders, school failure, friendship troubles, exam pressure, marriages fought for, and heavy-hearted divorce. Lives, usually hidden behind closed doors, are revealed as thunder grumbles above us.

When it's my turn to speak, it feels too brutal and disloyal to launch straight into our current mess so I track back to more innocent days: Dom, the golden-haired boy who grew up fascinated by animals, singing angelically in the bath, painting and cooking. How he threw himself into every new experience and filled our lives with laughter. Big on hugs and affection, everyone's friend. He was always mercurial but it never crossed my mind that he would struggle.

Even though the group feels safe and honest, I hesitate. I wonder how many others are doing the same, trying to protect their teens, scared that if they voice their worries out loud, they will be ostracised by the smug lucky ones who have a smoother path. I wrestle with this all the time at home, dropping hints to my friends that even Poirot might miss.

It feels like a huge leap of faith to tell near-strangers how Dom's teen years hit us like a whirlwind. We were lulled into a false sense of security by the rush of support when he came out as gay at fourteen, but his life rapidly turned sour. We've lived on tenterhooks ever since as he shrank against bullying in school during the day, then online 24/7, powerless in the face of the rising anxiety that resulted from it. Had anyone else seen their child shrink before their eyes into a pale shadow in the corner: hunched shoulders, eyes down, not even willing to go into assembly?

Encouraged by others sharing similar stories, I take the plunge, and describe how Dom's strategy was to face out his situation with bravado, and how this did nothing to endear him to his teachers, who I suspect then wrote him off as trouble and failed to gain his trust. I talk about how his friends disappeared and how he then got in with the kind of crowd that makes a mother tremble. I admit that my biggest fear is losing our rickety bridge to him, and so our conversations at home are laden with unspoken worries.

There are murmurs of recognition as I talk about how hard it is to get Dom to engage with anyone who might be able to help, how even raising the subject causes a massive scene. Lots of us know what it's like, I discover, to have a stubborn, struggling teenager at home.

Now I have started I can't stop, and talk about how hard it has been to keep Dom on the right side of the tracks and connected to us. How scared we are that he might walk out. That we've talked to his school but nothing is working; how in fact it has made it worse. So much so that Dom has asked us to stop going in. I explain that Dom doesn't want to move schools, that he wants to beat the bullies. I tell them about how I pace and fret whenever he goes out, anxious for his return and unable to release my breath until I hear his key in the lock.

My story peters out. No happy ending yet, but these women listen and it helps.

We have to stop talking as it takes all our energy to climb the hill back to the house. As we race against the curtain of rain we can see heading our way, I am comforted to know that I am not the only one. That yes, our tale has its ups and downs but, just like others before, we will come out of the teenage years into the bright sunny uplands of fledgling adults and a well-deserved rest.

Later, after a lazy afternoon drifting towards a champagne reception, I push back my chair from the dining table and appreciate how lucky we are to be here. It's good to see Jan relaxing with Kerry's husband, Steve. They too have that easy shorthand of friends who've known each other for years, meeting at school in 1977. There's so much love and laughter in the room and I think how fortunate Kerry is to have so many old friends. I don't think there's anyone in the room she's known for fewer than twenty years, and many for more than thirty. The glasses are catching the candlelight and reflecting it back in our faces as happy chatter rolls around the table, heavy with food and bottles. Kerry has insisted that we all come prepared to share a memory of our friendship with her and asks me to go first. Secretly pleased, I stand up, giddy on wine and the sense of belonging. I feel weirdly reckless telling the truth, but you're only fifty once.

Steadying myself on the back of my chair, I start by teasing Fish (my university nickname for Kerry) that I have not been able to find a story that I'm willing to share in front of our husbands. Getting into my flow, I explain to a 'home crowd' that Kerry is the friend I am most frightened of offending because I love her so much. Her high expectations of friendship mean I've seen many who don't make the cut, weeded out early on because when she does invest in friends, it's for the long term. That it's not so surprising Kerry is discerning about who she allows into her life as, in return, she gives back the fiercest loyalty a friend could wish for. How I'm hoping that, since I've been invited tonight and it's thirty-three years since we met, I passed the invisible test.

I glance at Fish, catch her eye to check I have done alright by her. I can see from the smile on her face that she's pleased despite protesting that she's really easy-going and tolerant. I take a big gulp of wine and settle back to enjoy the rest of the stories. In return for my speech, Kerry regales everyone with our time at Glastonbury Festival when we spent the weekend in a mud bath, cleaning our teeth with lager. She brings up my windsurfing attempts – or failures – when she was living at the beach in France on her year out and I paid her a visit. Those carefree times seem, in many ways, a long time ago, but the memories are still vivid, and those are still the people we readily identify with. The people we were before responsibility came to us.

Her voice cuts back through my thoughts.

'But the one thing I really, really love about Patti is her ability to find laughter in the direst of circumstances.'

I smile and think ruefully about how useful that's been over the last couple of years.

After the friends have all paid respects to the birthday girl, Cameron and Michaela, Kerry's children, stand up. I watch in admiration as they work the audience, joking and easy in their own skin. Shining with youth and beauty, they are part-charming, part-cheeky.

'I know I haven't always been the best son,' Cam says with all the confidence of someone who knows he's loved. He goes on to describe how he'd dived into a pond at a party, giving someone's priceless koi the fright of their lives, and Kerry's reaction to him arriving home dripping wet. 'But we do really appreciate all you do for us.' He comes to give his mum a hug.

I feel disloyal comparing but I know that Dom would not be able to do this. A shot of envy courses through my veins that Kerry has two such accomplished teens when I cannot even get mine to come out of his room on a bad day. With a jolt, I see up close just what a healthy teenager looks like and it is not what I see at home. I dab my eyes under the cover of the general emotion of the evening and resolve to speak to Dom when I get back. I'll try again to keep him on track for his new school, a fresh start for sixth form.

I don't for one minute begrudge Kerry her happiness and rose-tinted future, but I do wish my own life looked as simple.

CHAPTER TWO

Kerry

From Cough to Catastrophe

July/August 2017

'What's your strongest cough medicine? My son's going to Australia in two days' time.' I'm standing in our local pharmacy just before Cam goes off on a rugby tour, concerned about the poor sod who has to sit next to him hacking away on a plane for twenty-four hours.

The pharmacist hands over some medication and tells me, 'If it's viral, it could take six weeks to go.' I think nothing of it. I am far more worried about him breaking his neck in the scrum. So much so that I want to cling to him, savour every moment of my healthy, robust seventeen-year-old on the cusp of the rest of his life. When it's time for him to leave, I try not to spoil the send-off at school by crying but, in the end, I give him a quick hug and sit snivelling in the car while the coach pulls away.

Three weeks pass without incident and I'm relieved when Steve picks up Cam from Heathrow in one piece. Because of a mix-up over Cam's return dates, I'm still on holiday in Greece with our daughter, Michaela, and some friends. It's been one of those rare, blissful weeks of doing nothing, a little oasis in the busyness of life, catching up with Sharon, a friend from my days as a holiday rep in Italy nearly thirty years ago. We're completely relaxed in each other's company – she knew me before I airbrushed myself into a responsible parent. I've just delivered a new novel to my editor, work pressure is off and the summer is stretching ahead with a family holiday in Sardinia to look forward to.

I receive a text from Steve two days before I'm due home, telling me he's taking Cam to the doctor's because his cough hasn't gone yet.

Is it bad? I write, thinking, *Get some Benylin, I'm sure it will be fine,* and internally rolling my eyes at the hypochondriac husband.

Later Steve texts to say, *Doc thinks it's a chest infection. He's got some antibiotics.* I go back to reading *Small Great Things* and wonder what time it's acceptable to start drinking mojitos.

When I finally get home, Cam meets us at the airport and I hug him until he shakes me off. I've missed him. I don't really notice the cough. He still seems tired though and goes to bed at 8.30 p.m. Neither of us has ever been good at getting over jetlag.

The next day, Cam and I go shopping for a suit for his return to school in the upper sixth. He's gone down a waist size. We laugh about how chubby he'd been in primary school and how I'd had to buy the plus-size school trousers from Marks & Spencer. Over lunch, he tells me about Australia, the parties he went to, the families he met. While he's chatting, I keep having little bursts of pride that he's confident enough to travel to the other side of the world, stay with people he doesn't know and embrace every minute of it. When we get home, Steve asks me about the cough and I tell him it seemed better. We smile at each other. Steve says, 'Phew.'

By Friday afternoon, Cam is still coughing and Steve reminds me that the doctor said if the cough hadn't completely gone in a week, we needed to go back. I don't want to find myself standing in an Italian hospital rather than sitting on my sun lounger in a couple of weeks so I offer to take him for another check-up.

The doctor examines him and says, 'He might have picked up an odd bacteria abroad.' She hesitates. 'You could take him to A&E for a chest X-ray.'

My middle-class, mustn't-waste-NHS-resources-unnecessarily sanctimony kicks in. 'I'd feel ridiculous going to A&E for a cough.'

She frowns. 'It's up to you. I can give you a different antibiotic and you can come back after the weekend so I can see how you're getting on or you could go to A&E tonight.'

I take the prescription for the antibiotics. When I tell Steve, he says, 'I'm going to take him to A&E.'

Cam grumbles about it being 'such a waste of time' and privately I agree, but Steve is adamant. Three hours later at 10 p.m., he calls me. 'They've X-rayed his chest and want to keep him in. I think you'd better come down and bring an overnight bag and some food.'

He can't tell me anything more. The first tendrils of unease start to unfurl. I wonder if he has pneumonia or an acute chest infection. I stuff some clothes in a bag and Michaela and I nip to the garage for sandwiches and sweets.

At the hospital, Cam is tucked away in what seems like a holding area – not A&E proper but not a ward. He seems fine, scoffing up sweets and eating crisps. Cam is laughing, telling us how he fainted at the sight of the needle and how the nurse had been all irritated and 'a big rugby player like you'. Steve explains that she'd told him off for not doing anything about Cam's cough until now. Frankly, I'm surprised how quickly we've done something. If it hadn't been for Steve, Cam's cough might not have reached the top of my priority volcano for another month or two. I hope they're not going to tell us that he can't fly a week tomorrow. I reassure myself that once they get the right antibiotics into him, he'll be fine.

We wait until midnight when a harassed doctor comes and says, 'We've looked at the X-ray and there's an unusual mass on his chest. That's worrying because we don't know what it is.'

The word that stands out for me is 'mass'. 'Mass' doesn't sound good. What would cause a mass? Does an infection cause a mass?

'What could it be?' I ask.

The doctor answers, 'We need to run some more bloods and get him a scan.' The word 'scan' registers loud and clear. It's one of those ugly words capable of changing a situation from easily fixable to potentially serious. It makes my stomach lurch and list and takes me to places I don't want to consider. He won't be drawn on possibilities. 'We'll get him a bed on a ward and we'll see you in the morning.'

'I'm not going anywhere,' I say.

'I don't think we have any parent–child rooms available.'

'I'll sleep in a chair.' I fold my arms and know with absolute certainty I will not be leaving that hospital when my son has just been told he has 'an unusual mass' on his chest.

The other two leave. We hug. No one cries. No one really believes it is that serious.

The next day is my dad's eightieth birthday party. He's arranged it around Cam's Australia trip and our holiday. And here I am at 4 a.m. on a Z-bed in a side room with a son who might be seriously ill. There are shouts, old men shouts, for the nurse. The sound of sensible shoes clacking along the lino. The beeps of monitors. And Cam breathing next to me. Fear rushes in, as powerful as water through a sluice gate. I reassure myself that Cam has only ever had two days off school in his life. Barely ever had a cold. There's no reason why he would suddenly get something serious. Do they think it's cancer? It can't be cancer. He's been playing rugby in Australia for three weeks, for God's sake. I spoke to him while he was away, several times. He didn't mention feeling ill. I can't remember a cough.

I ask Steve to phone my dad and let him know we can't make the party. 'Tell him that Cam is in hospital for a chest infection. Let's not worry him unnecessarily.' I can't phone him myself, can't hear his voice, can't become a child leaning on my dad when my need – my son's need for me – to be a parent who won't crumble has never been greater. Dad will be really upset we're not there. I push away the image of all my family and his friends laughing and drinking while we stand on this precipice not knowing whether a hand will shoot out to pull us back from the edge or shove us right into the abyss.

We spend Saturday in an unsatisfactory limbo. We're lucky enough to get a CT scan but because someone ticked the wrong box, they can only see part of what they need to look at. Steve and I sit shaking our heads, telling ourselves that it can't be that bad. Cam doesn't even look particularly ill. Just a bit tired. I practically beg one of the nurses to give me her best educated guess. Reluctantly she puts me out of my misery. 'It's not definite, but it's probably some sort of lymphoma.'

I don't tell Cam.

Saturday 12 August, 20.53
Hi Pat and Jan

Just thought you should know that Cam is currently in hospital with suspected lymphoma. We thought he had a chest infection after Australia and we are completely devastated. I have never felt so sick with fear, never even understood that concept (though thought I did). We don't know for sure yet, more CT scans tomorrow. Just wanted to give you the heads up that we might not be around for the weekend we had planned in November.

Trying to clear the decks for what lies ahead.
Xx

Sunday 13 August, 0.53
Hi Fish

Jan and I just picked up the message at the same time. We are so shocked to hear that news and cannot imagine what you must be going through. Please let us know if we can help in ANY way and don't even think about November… one day at a time.

Hope that the tests prove to be good news and please let us know. Want to be able to support you all as best we can. Thinking of you and sending all our love and I'll give you a call tomorrow.

Xx

Sunday 13 August, 7.00
Hi Fish

Not often me that can do this but if you think it would help, I could be with you by this afternoon. Let me know.

Pat xx

Sunday 13 August, 7.27

Actually, that sounds very appealing if you are sure and if you promise not to cry. You CAN'T cry or I will crumble.

Kerry xx

By Sunday afternoon, it becomes apparent that going into hospital on a Friday night is designed to push parents with a seriously ill child right to the fringes of insanity. We can't move forward until he has another scan. There's no one about who can make the scan happen, now, now please, so we know whether we can quell the terror that initially was blowing a few scraps of paper along the pavement and is now ripping tiles off the roofs and turning over cars. Steve and I sit. Sit and sit. He paces and ruffles the nurses' feathers, unwilling to accept that we're not going to find out anything today. I dip in and out, smoothing things over like the sweeper in a game of curling in case we drop to the bottom of the priority list for bad behaviour.

I am so relieved when Pat texts from the hospital car park. An excuse to get up, to leave this little room where worry perches on every surface like a big black crow. I fold myself into her, swearing out all my fears, letting the words that I've been squashing down reach the air, afraid to say even to Steve in case he agrees with me. Someone with a bit more emotional distance to help steady the ship. Steve goes home to look after Michaela. I'm guiltily glad not to have to look into the mirror of his pain for a few hours. Cam, however, is pretty blasé, more worried about missing our holiday to Sardinia if he doesn't get out of hospital by next Saturday rather than the prospect of finding out he might bloody die.

Pat produces a pack of cards and I love her for carrying the conversation when all my words sound false and over-bright.

Cam doesn't want me to stay the night. And as we embark on another game of Cheat, he says, 'After this, you can go.'

'Three sevens.'

'Cheat!'

I can't leave him. I don't want him to be awake at 3 a.m. with no one to talk to.

'Two aces.'

'Three jacks.'

'Three fours.'

What if these are my countdown hours? What if in two months' time I look back and think, *Why didn't I stay?*, breathing him in, imprinting him in my mind to carry with me when I am without him.

The game finishes. I jump to my feet. 'Right, love. Give me a hug. Sleep well. See you in the morning.'

Pat and I make it out into the corridor before I double over.

I can't eat, only drink. We stay up late glugging back wine and I'm grateful to have her there to dilute the intensity of the terror batting backwards and forwards between Steve and me.

On Monday, when it becomes obvious that it's too late for any scans to happen, I beg the matron to let him come home for an hour for a shower. She nods but tells me not to tell anyone so that we don't lose our room and, consequently, our place in the priority pecking order. Cam and I scuttle out of the hospital like a couple of battery hens making a bid for freedom. I cannot believe the sun is shining. Doesn't it realise the world is ending? Cam looks grey in the light and I tell myself that anyone who'd been sitting in a hospital room for three days would be looking pretty wan by now. He doesn't speak on the way home and I don't know how to reach him. All the variations of 'I know you're only seventeen and you might have cancer but let's look on the bright side till we know' gather in my throat like a hairball. I put the radio on, then switch it off. I don't want to hear anyone else's words about love and loss when my own are reverberating around my head.

The whole house is unsettled by having him home and knowing he has to leave again. Pat chats, asks him if he can sleep at the hospital. He talks about how frightening it is, hearing the men shouting for the nurse. 'I'm afraid they'll wander into my room.' We decide that he needs headphones to block out the noise. 'What's the budget?'

'There isn't one.' Suddenly all the 'money doesn't grow on trees' arguments seem futile when I don't know what the future holds.

For the first time that day he smiles. Bose headphones on their way. 'You did say no budget.'

The next day I leave Pat in charge of food shopping and dog walking. I go to the hospital early because I don't want Cam to wake up on his own. I creep in while he's still asleep and sit looking at his feet. That little mole on his second toe. I look, really look, at his ears, his nose, the way he sleeps, has always slept with his hands behind his head as though he's sunbathing. I've only been back from Greece a week. That person who wore a bikini and slid down the aqua slides in a rubber ring seems unrecognisable now.

Steve arrives in time for the consultant's round and not long afterwards there is a flurry of action. Lots of doctorish people, four or five, with lots of faffing about introducing people and asking whether it is okay for the intern to be there. I don't care about body count. I care about scans. One of the doctors says the 'mass' on the X-ray could be a swollen thymus. I've never heard of it but thought it might become my new best friend if it wasn't cancer. Then he throws us a glittering lifebelt. 'It might be glandular fever.' Of course. Lovely glandular fever. My brother had that. He's still here. Brilliant. The little knot of anxiety loosens, a half-twist back towards normality. I briefly imagine being in our kitchen, laughing about the time we thought Cam had cancer and it turned out he'd been snogging too many girls. Then the golden words. 'He'll be taken down for a scan this morning.'

The consultant is about to leave then says, 'I gather there's been some confusion about the scans.'

I'm embarrassed, don't want to be seen to be troublesome now I've got what I want. 'We were a bit frustrated by the delay.'

He frowns and tells me they don't really count a few days as a delay.

I'm not embarrassed now. 'But it's not your seventeen-year-old son who might have cancer. To us, a few days feels like the end of the world.'

He inclines his head. I feel as though he thinks that our expectations are ridiculous. And I wonder what would have happened if we hadn't made a fuss. Would we still be waiting?

Everything moves quickly. Cam goes for a CT scan. 'They put something funny in the drip. I thought I was going to wet myself.' He seems relaxed and far more interested in when the

Gucci trainers (I know, I know) I've let him order will arrive than what the scan might show.

A school friend turns up and hugs him. 'Poor old Cam.' I'm touched by his ease with it all, by how he speaks to Cam normally, teases him, laughs with him, when I'm already finding it difficult to talk to him without thinking of him as a patient, as someone ill, who must be asked, 'How are you feeling?' twenty times an hour. His lovely rugby teacher from school joins them. We dispense with the usual Mr and Mrs-ing, especially when I drop an F-bomb recounting the botched scan of the weekend. I see his face shift into a 'That's not the language I usually hear from school parents.' I can't muster up a blush. I wonder if I'll ever care about anything other than Cam getting well again. Steve and I take the opportunity to sit outside. He buys me a salad, encourages me to eat. I can't get anything down apart from Percy Pigs.

Later, a new consultant comes in. He nods and talks about the scan, describing the size of the mass in the chest and in his lymph nodes. And then Cam asks the question we are both shying away from and wanting to know the answer to. 'Have I got cancer?'

In a bedside manner that does not fit with the scenario I'd imagined of 'If you'd just like to take a seat, I'd like to break the news to you very gently and suggest we don't jump to conclusions', he shrugs and says, 'Eight out of ten cancer, two out of ten, not. Tomorrow a biopsy.'

That is how my seventeen-year-old son, this boy who still has to be reminded to clean his teeth, who can't find his sports kit without my intervention, is told he might have an illness that could kill him.

And off the consultant trots, leaving us in no doubt that we are just one family in a long list of people he has to charm that day.[1]

1　Cam loved this consultant because he was the only one that didn't give him any 'bullshit'. Personally, I wasn't averse to a tiny sugar-coating of bullshit.

By Wednesday, Pat has to leave our lives and go back to her own. We hug. The sort of hug infused with love that friends who've known each other for years give each other when they know it's only going to get worse and there just aren't any words to make it better. I don't want her to go. I don't want to lose the buffer she creates between everyone in the family, stopping our misery feeding off each other's. Without her there, I'm frightened all our dark thoughts will distil down into the intense despair we're just managing to keep at bay.

Back at the hospital, a porter comes to wheel Cam to the biopsy. He could have walked and the whole wheelchair thing seems ridiculous, another nudge in the 'you are seriously ill' direction that we have yet to accept. Cam doesn't really know what a biopsy is beyond 'they're going to take some tissue samples' but he's frightened. Fuck it. I'm frightened. The porter gabbles on, chatting about music. He's trying to be nice but I just want him to stop, to let us gather ourselves for what lies ahead.

In a small voice, Cam asks him, 'What do they do in a biopsy?' Cam is terrified of needles and I see the porter about to launch into a 'They get the biggest pointiest needle known to mankind…'

I'm walking behind the wheelchair and tap him on the shoulder, making a slicing motion across my neck and he freezes. 'Um, I'm not sure. The doctor will tell you.'

The sight of the radiologist immediately reassures me. Old enough to *know*, young enough to have a steady hand. He's chatty and friendly as he brings up the image of Cam's lymph nodes on the screen and decides he can go in through the neck – a good thing apparently. The nurse says, 'There's going to be a little sting, like a wasp, as the anaesthetic goes in.'

The procedure begins and Cam starts moaning in pain. Despite my best efforts, tears roll down my face. I lean back behind the nurse so he can't see. The nurse says, 'Maybe more like a hornet.'

I want to be away from these insects, I want to hold Cam's hand, I want to stop crying and be braver for my son. And I just can't.

Instead, I rear up at intervals to say in a skipping-through-the-daisies voice I have never used before, 'You're doing brilliantly, love, nearly there…' before folding into silent sobs.

Eventually, after the third tissue harpooning expedition, the radiologist says, 'I'm pretty sure it's Hodgkin's lymphoma. Four to six sessions of chemotherapy and you'll be able to get on with your life.'

The bar has indeed dropped to a new low that my reaction is one of joy, not despair. Steve's googling means we already know that Hodgkin's is the cancer to get, the one with the best chance of remission. Lucky us.

In the afternoon, the consultant of the marvellous bedside manner confirms that it is indeed Hodgkin's lymphoma. He alludes to a couple of things that didn't look quite like Hodgkin's but says that in the main, 'It walks like Hodgkin's and talks like Hodgkin's.' He mentions something else it could be but we don't question him further. Confirmation of cancer alone is enough to take in, along with the news that Cam will have to go to the Royal Marsden the next day for a PET scan, a full-body scan that will show detailed information about how far the disease has spread. Then chemo will start.

Cam asks, 'Will I lose my hair?'

Without missing a single beat the consultant says, 'Yes, you will have a squeaky, white bald head.'

I want to grab him by his tie and say, 'Do you want to dress that up at all for my child, who is just taking in the massive news that he has cancer?'

But apparently not, because he then goes on to say, 'And when it grows back it might be white or curly.'

In the afternoon, Cam and I are allowed home for a few hours. He's specifically asked to see one of my oldest, funniest friends, Bev. We had our first babies within weeks of each other and Cam adores her. They've always made each other laugh and she's dropped everything to drive two hours to bring a treasure trove of biscuits, cake and chocolate. But after the initial delight of seeing her, Cam lies on the sofa, headphones on, morose and monosyllabic, and we don't know how to reach him. I'm so glad she's here, so grateful to be able to talk to someone without having to be brave. When the phone goes, I tell her to get rid of the caller. I'm not in the mood to go over what's happening for the tenth time that day. But she hands me the phone and the bloke on the other end introduces himself as being from 'patient transport'. I clarify that I'm the patient's mother, not the hospital.

'Yours was the only number on the form.'

I'm too slow to point out that a quick google would probably deliver the hospital number he needs. He says, 'We don't cover the Royal Marsden any more so we can't take the boy to his scan.'

'Who can, then?'

'I don't know who does it now.'

So we cannot start treatment until we've had the full body scan and we're arguing about who's driving there? I phone the matron on Cam's ward. She reassures me that she'll sort it. When I take Cam back that evening she tells me that she's booked 'private transport'.

I go to bed but can't sleep. I'm worried that there'll be a mix up, that the right transport won't be there by eight o'clock. At 5 a.m. I give up trying to sleep and drive to the hospital. The night staff are surprised to see me. I ask them to check the travel arrangements again. A nurse reads 'Booked for nine o'clock.'

I shake my head. 'No, the scan is at nine o'clock.' I know they've had to fight for a slot for Cam, that the PET scans have a waiting list. We can't miss this.

She stands with her fingers crossed in front of my face and says, 'Fingers crossed they know to come a bit earlier.'

That poor nurse cops my grief and frustration. 'Fingers crossed? My son has cancer and I don't feel like crossing my bloody fingers!'

She immediately promises that as soon as the office opens at seven she will ring to check. I know, of course, it's not her fault. I don't recognise myself. I'm usually the one running about apologising for being a nuisance.

In the meantime, another nurse brings me tea and toast. 'Keep your strength up. He needs you.' I'm not the sort of woman who would have needed smelling salts in Victorian times. I'm sturdy, robust and my kids tell me they'll put 'Just *get on* with it' on my gravestone. But I can't get that bit of toast down.

By half past seven there's no progress. I lurk in Cameron's room, peering through the little glass diamond in the door at an increasingly wide circle of nurses shaking their heads. The rage that builds inside me is frightening. I walk out to the nurses' station. I stand with my arms folded and, in the calmest voice I can manage, I say, 'If there's no transport here in the next ten minutes, I will drive Cami myself.'

They shake their heads. 'It's not procedure for patients to drive themselves.'

'I don't give a damn about procedure.'

The head nurse tells me she's ordering a 'blue light'. The relief is so great, I feel a physical sensation of tension draining away. In fact, two lots of transport arrive; there's a kerfuffle over who is going to take us but in the end we set off in a van with two paramedics discussing their hangovers. As we drive down the high street, I see people I know wandering along, walking into Marks & Spencer, leading normal lives.

I concentrate on breathing in and out, trying to hold it all together. Cam says, 'Mum, stop with the worried face. It's incon-

venient, but it's just a blip and I'll be fine.' A blip. God bless the
teenager. It feels like the end of the world to me.

When we arrive for the PET scan, radioactive glucose is pumped
into Cam's body and then we have to wait for it to circulate for an
hour. Apparently, the sugar is attracted to tumours and will light
up on the scan where there is cancer. I imagine his whole body
illuminating like a perverse Ready Brek advert. Bones? Liver? Brain?
How bad can it be? Cam gets upset when the cannula goes in and
I sit there as he puts his headphones on, singing out loud to music
I can't hear, his voice sometimes descending into sobbing, then
singing again. I've never felt more helpless and unable to comfort.
Like me, when Cam's stressed or scared, he just wants to sink
down into himself and not have everyone fussing and wringing
their hands. It takes every single bit of self-control not to run over
to the couch and touch him, hold onto him. My mind runs on a
loop, thinking back to all the moments when he was little when
I hoped he'd go to sleep so I could get some work done, read the
paper, have five minutes in my own head. When I'd grumpily
tried to get him to read Biff and Chip for the fiftieth time while
he hung upside down on the sofa practising his Scottish accent,
not giving a hoot about Floppy the dog. How different I would
have been if I'd known that we might only have him for seventeen
years, instead of the decades I'd taken for granted.

Eventually a doctor takes him through to the scanner – a great
big doughnut machine – where he is fed in on a conveyor belt.
The man working the scanner tells me the results will be at the
hospital by four o'clock. I try to read his face. What could he
see? Does he know already that my son will die? He doesn't give
anything away. Poker face par excellence. We get back into the
ambulance and return to the hospital.

Thankfully, Cam's rugby teacher visits in the afternoon. We've
dispensed with all that formal stuff and hug. He joins the elite

band of people I will never be able to hear a bad word about again. I slip off to the cafe. I answer a few emails including one from someone who'd like me to read her book. I explain that my son has been diagnosed with cancer, and as I'm sure she'll appreciate I have to conserve my energy for looking after him. The reply comes straight back that she's so sorry to hear my bad news but 'do you know any agents you could recommend?'

It's the closest I've come to laughing all day.

CHAPTER THREE

Kerry

From Cough to Chemo

18–24 August 2017

The PET scan shows that the tumour hasn't spread below his spleen, which is a tick in the good news box. And we're going to be transferred to the Royal Marsden with the specialist teenage cancer unit as soon as a bed is free. We hang around all day Friday waiting. I keep walking past the nurses' station, in case they've forgotten about us. The matron tells me that the consultant has been working round the clock out of hours to move Cam's treatment along. Suddenly his brusque manner doesn't seem to matter. If he's moving mountains to get us from admission to chemo in just over a week, then going forwards, he can be as blunt as he likes.

But no bed for us at the Marsden. I'm ashamed of how little empathy I have for the other poor parents whose children are in those beds, how selfish this whole process is making me. I only care about Cam.

We're sent off to another hospital instead to get chemo underway. Steve, Cam and I navigate new territory – we're no longer on a ward for mixed ages and ailments but on a ward for seriously ill children where every parent looks as though it's years since they slept. The nurse takes one look at Cam and says, 'You don't look ill enough to be here.' But sadly he is. We quickly learn that we've got a few more hurdles to overcome before we can get on with pumping him full of poison.

The doctor tells Cam that he needs to think about fertility preservation because the chemotherapy he's going to have could make him infertile. Cam nods but I get the sense that none of this really means anything to him. Having a problem in ten or fifteen years' time seems like a luxury right now. After the doctor has left, I ask him if he understands what 'fertility preservation' entails. He rolls his eyes. 'They're not going to stick a needle in my balls, are they?'

I laugh, explain and tell him it might be the most enjoyable part of the whole treatment. He puts his head in his hands. 'That's so embarrassing.'

For a moment, I think he won't go through with it. 'Do you think you'll want children later on?' As I say it, I'm finding it hard to imagine him sitting down with a girlfriend and telling her he might not be able to father children. More than hard to imagine, I'm afraid to imagine it. That's the odd thing about this disease. We've stopped thinking about the future completely. Just today, tomorrow and when the chemo will start.

'Yes, I think I do want children.' He sighs, but it's good humoured, just another thing to get through.

Yet again, his courage and total lack of self-pity humble me. The chief nurse specialist is reluctant to discuss any of this with me and I'm reduced to saying things like, 'I understand there's a plan for tomorrow morning. What would be a good time for me to visit?' I really don't want to blunder in at an inopportune moment. My man-child is making life-changing decisions and they seem affronted that I want to understand what's going on.

It might well be that the NHS considers anyone over sixteen an adult but this shit is big and for someone who can't legally drink in a pub yet, it seems quite a lot to be navigating when your mother still buys your underpants.

The next morning Cam phones. 'I've done it.'

It doesn't seem appropriate to ask how it went but Cam starts laughing. 'First of all, they came in and asked if I wanted any "material" to help.' The mind boggles at what the NHS might provide. I try not to imagine how many men a porn magazine might have to service for the taxpayers to have got their money's worth. 'Then the man who changes the sheets on the bed stood guard on the door while I did it. Afterwards I had to tick a box to say the whole sample had gone into the pot. I felt like saying, "No, and the windows need a bit of a wipe."'

Thank God for humour. Thank God for teenage hormones able to perform in the least salubrious of circumstances. Thank God for my stoic son because without him dragging us through with his relentless optimism, goodness knows how far we could fall. The only time I see him break down other than when he is in terrible pain is when he realises that despite just being made rugby captain of the first fifteen – the dream he's had all through school – he won't be able to play. 'Why me, why now, Mum? I was flying.'

I have no answer.

Before chemo can start, he needs a PICC line – a permanent line that can feed the poison to the right place. The chief nurse specialist assures us that he's done the procedure on small babies, that it's quite straightforward. Steve and Michaela go and lurk in the cafe – our second home – while I stay with Cam for the 'straightforward procedure' that leads to him crying and screaming while I sit on my hands, desperate to reach out, to make it all stop. We all breathe a sigh of relief when it's in but that's just the beginning of the nightmare ahead. Because the chemo is so toxic, the nurse needs to make sure there's 'bleed back', i.e. that blood can be drawn back out of the tube to prove it's in the right place. The chemo is supposed to start that day but the nurse isn't satisfied that the PICC line is where it should be. The suggestion for solving that is for Cam to move his arm about to get things moving. He doesn't like the feel of the tube and just seeing the end of it poking out makes him feel sick. He point blank refuses to move his arm. The nurse explains he has to. I explain that he has to, feeling myself teetering between gentle persuasion and grabbing his hand and yanking it up and down for all I'm worth. But he won't budge. His stubbornness makes me feel as though I might start hurling about blood pressure monitors and urine bottles before keeling over with the utter frustration of it all.

That day and the ones that follow have a horribly predictable pattern. Despite various attempts every few hours, they can't start the chemo because there's no bleed back. Cam is spectacularly unconcerned, far more interested in which friends are coming to see him than jiggling his arm about so we can crack on with the treatment that might save his life. Every day, ridiculously late in the evening he goes for an X-ray to check the PICC line is where it should be, but by then there are very few doctors around to give the go ahead. Several times his chemo starts at three in the morning by which time I've had to go home before I make everything worse by exploding. Cam doesn't want me there. He doesn't want to be reminded of how bad it is. He lives instead for the groups of girls, turning up with sweets and cards and teddies, the lads filling him in on rugby pre-season gossip. Every evening a posse of his friends arrive and I sit in the cafe downstairs, leaving to the sound of giggling and Cam talking about his radioactive wee.

*

One evening, I completely unravel, unable to cope with the 'Will we, won't we be able to do chemo tonight?' Cam is furious with me. He's barely seen me cry before and I think it frightens him. I'm furious with myself. I want to be strong and hate myself for the message I'm giving out to my seventeen-year-old, who's missing out on summer barbecues, whose friends are texting pictures from parties he can't attend: 'You're the one with cancer but *I* can't cope.' I hide in a little room down the corridor waiting to feel calm again. I never do.

Eventually he texts me about ten o'clock, asking me to go back in. His friend looks utterly appalled as I creep in looking like roadkill. Mothers are supposed to be in control. Cam tells me to go home. I sob out to the nurses' station, wanting to check who is in charge of Cam overnight. Their faces carry the weariness of dealing with emotional parents. I've seen how young, how sick, some of the children are on this ward. Cam isn't the worst, but I can't leave without knowing who has got his back. I set off, getting lost in a diversion because a road is closed and sit in total desperation because I don't even know whether I'm heading towards London or away from it. My crap phone can't bring up maps. I've never felt lonelier in my life. When I get home, Pat's husband, Jan, is there, keeping Steve company. I burst in sobbing before the dynamics of our friendship kick in: we always laugh, always have done in every circumstance. I make my bad day funny, a story to entertain and in doing so, I feel myself lift out of deep despair.

CHAPTER FOUR

Kerry

The News Gets Worse

25 August–4 September 2017

On 25 August, Cam is allowed to come home. I can't wait. I've had to steel myself to go into his bedroom, forcing away thoughts of whether it would become a shrine to him if he dies. I try not to imagine the rugby ball sitting on the windowsill faded by the sun in twenty years' time. None of these thoughts are helpful but I don't know how not to have them. When Steve arrives back with Cam, there's a flatness about my husband, rather than the joy I'd expected. 'They've had another look at the biopsy. It's not Hodgkin's but Grey Zone – a really rare cancer that's halfway between Hodgkin's and Non-Hodgkin's. It was only discovered in 2008.'

'Can they treat it?'

Steve nods. 'The prognosis is still good.'

It's the way he hesitates on 'still'.

'But not as good?'

He shakes his head. 'About eighty per cent rather than ninety-five.'

If you were betting, they'd be great odds. But a one-in-five chance of my child dying? Steve goes off to research world experts in Grey Zone and to work out how much money we'd need for treatment in America if that's what we have to do. I sit outside the bathroom door, irrationally afraid that Cam will die in the shower.

Life has stopped for us. It becomes clear that I can't go back to work in the near future. Steve and I meet with the headmaster to see if we can keep Cam at school, overwhelming him with our new knowledge. We have to be told if he's been near anyone with chicken pox; he needs specially treated blood if he is in an accident and requires a blood transfusion; he'll be susceptible to colds. It's the autumn term. I can't see how he's going to get through this last year of his A-levels. Suddenly those grades we've been banging on about, the necessity of working hard to get to university, seem utterly irrelevant. But the school is very supportive and promises they'll do all they can to help. Weirdly, for the first time in his whole life, Cam can't wait to go back to school. 'I hate being at home. It just makes me think about being ill.'

We try not to take it personally. He doesn't even seem very ill, or not ill in the way I'd imagined a person with cancer. We've been instructed to take his temperature regularly – too high or too low and we need to get to A&E immediately in case it's the start of an infection. I've never even owned a thermometer and invest in a great big all-singing all-dancing ear trumpet, and chase round the house after him, ramming it into his ear at every opportunity. No wonder he doesn't want to be here.

At the weekend he tells us he's going to a party. He drives off, promising to be careful, one of the many evenings I have to fight the urge to forbid him to go out, struggling to let his need to live his life while he still can triumph over my desire to plant him on the sofa where I can see him, secretly taking photos in case they're the last ones I have. I ask him to text me to let me know he's okay. About ten, he messages. *Having a great time. Don't worry.*

We relax. Then a text arrives: *My back is agony, get the gate open for me, I need to go to hospital.*

He can barely climb out of the car. Steve rushes him to A&E, while I stay with Michaela, wondering whether the cancer has spread somewhere else in his body. I doze, with various updates arriving from Steve about X-rays, morphine, waiting, the endless waiting. They come home at 6 a.m., with no resolution for his back but relief that it doesn't appear to be related to cancer. Everyone sleeps for a bit until the morphine wears off and Cam starts to cry out in pain. By lunchtime, I take him back to the hospital where he collapses on the floor in A&E. I show the receptionist our fast-track chemo card that shoots us to the front of the queue – every cloud and all that – and there's a flurry of activity. Cam loses a shoe as he falls and a woman I am too flustered to thank properly picks it up. I'm quickly discovering there's the kindness of strangers everywhere. It's a Sunday but it's busy. There's a man in the cubicle next door describing a problem with his penis at the top of his voice in an upper-class accent. There's an old, drunk woman shouting at a black nurse that she doesn't like 'her sort'. The nurse keeps calm, polite and firm. Yet again, I pay silent homage to all these nurses and doctors doing their best for people who insult them. More morphine later, we're sent home.

Cam is supposed to start the new chemo regime, the one that fits his latest diagnosis, at the Royal Marsden the following day. We arrive exhausted at the Children's and Young People's Centre in Sutton. He can barely walk.[2] A nurse scoops him up, takes charge and from that moment on, I feel the responsibility of keeping him alive transfer from me, the amateur bumbling about with a thermometer, to the experts who know what they are doing. It's all so smooth, so professional. There's always an

---

2 The back problem turned out to be four vertebrae out of place, the muscles either side of the spine weakened by three weeks in bed and finished off by vigorous dancing…

answer, someone is always on it already, whatever question I ask. They pump Cam full of morphine and start the chemo. A nurse tells me that one of Cam's drugs, Rituximab, is a miracle drug. Like a child telling herself that Father Christmas is real, I cling onto the word 'miracle'. Within minutes, Cam has an allergic reaction to it and starts rigoring (shaking uncontrollably), yelling in pain as the spasms hurt his back. One nurse holds him down, another shouts down the corridor for drugs. The urgency of their response frightens me. As I sit petrified in the corner, the nurse tells me to call my husband. I shake my head. 'I don't want him driving here in a panic. I'm stronger than I look.'

But really I was thinking, *You'll either sort it or he'll be dead by the time Steve gets here.*

Eventually the horrible shaking stops but then his temperature goes above 38 degrees. To make sure there's no infection, they find a bed on the teenage cancer ward and keep him in.

In some ways, it's like a luxury hotel – a music room, state of the art computers, games, books, a huge TV. Cam stays on a ward while they find a way to get the Rituximab into him. When I comment on how gorgeous the young nurse is looking after him, he deadpans, 'Mum, she's seen me pee into a bottle and shit in a cardboard box. It's not a great start really, is it?' We both kill ourselves laughing. One of the huge bonuses of him being in hospital is that I'm not sleeping on red alert and feel more rested than I have for days.

We are invited to a brunch for patients and their carers. Cam hesitates on the threshold as he sees the other teenagers with their bald heads, the promised bacon butty no longer so appealing. He hasn't yet accepted that he's 'one of them' and, for the moment, he still has his hair. I meet a few other parents wearing the same lacerated look that unites us. Some of their children have leukaemia and are much sicker than Cam, but all of them are much further down the road than me with their stories of stem cell transplants, isolation rooms, their children living at the hospital for weeks on end. One mother is waiting for some stem cells to be flown in from abroad, worrying that the donor will change his mind or have an accident on the way to the hospital. She tells me the thing she hates most is being worried all the time. The thing she misses most is finishing work early and having a coffee with her friends. It's such a small thing but I really understand. That loss of ever feeling worry-free. The realisation dawns that there's no quick fix, that our old life has gone and whether it ever comes back is in the lap of the gods. I feel an overwhelming longing for my former self.

The night before the autumn term starts, they finally manage to get the Rituximab into him and we are sent home. Dressed in his new suit, he drives off with Michaela the next morning as though nothing has changed. I bite back the 'Don't stand next to anyone with a cold; keep washing your hands.' I don't leave home all day in case at the very moment he needs me, I don't have a mobile signal. I rub down the kitchen windows and paint the frames to stop me going mad, feeling weirdly resentful that everyone else is back at school or work but I'm here, untethered like a balloon not knowing where to land. My old, multi-faceted identity – wife, mother, daughter, author – is streamlined into just one.

The mother of a son with cancer.

Practical things that might help navigate the world of childhood cancer – Kerry

I'm the worst person to ask about any actual medical knowledge of cancer as I deliberately stepped away from Google or any real investigation into Cam's condition on the grounds that I didn't want to discover anything that would worry me any more than I already was. It was most unlike me to be head in the sand but that was my coping mechanism. But I did learn these practical things, which I hope are helpful.

- Early on, I had to decide that I wasn't going to let my son die because I was too polite to question people who obviously knew much more than me. I still felt really uncomfortable asking for more clarification or hassling for scans but I got over that by seeing it as an investment in keeping him alive.
- Make sure you ask which medication side effect of the many that they warn you about is most likely. We ended up in A&E thinking that the cancer had spread to Cam's abdomen because he was doubled over in pain when, in fact, it was constipation caused by Vincristine, one of the chemo drugs. An incident henceforth known as 'turdgate'.
- When children turn sixteen, they are considered adults in the eyes of the NHS and some doctors can be reluctant to let the parent sit in on conversations. Personally, I think sixteen is too young to be discussing fertility preservation and treatment options without a bit of parental input – thoughts about fertility (or anything else that seems a long way away)

at sixteen are bound to be different from a thirty-year-old in a stable relationship. When my mum went into hospital at eighty, she was actively encouraged to bring someone with her. It's best to discuss this with your child beforehand so if there's an issue they can say confidently that they want you there.

- In our experience, the chemo was always carried out sitting in an armchair. If the treatment is long, it's worth asking if a bed is available. Cam slept through most of his. I always took food and drinks as I never liked leaving him. I also optimistically brought a book though I never managed to read anything, just sat there in a daze.

- Buy a year's season ticket to the hospital car park. Probably cheaper in the long run and saves faffing about with coins in the rain after a long day of chemo.

- Steve and I asked for a meeting with the oncologist without Cam there. We wanted to ask about treatments and discuss some of our worries without making him feel as though we thought he was going to die.

- Make sure you know who your CNS (clinical nurse specialist) is. Ours was absolutely brilliant and answered our emails very promptly, saving us hours of worry.

- Take advantage of any post-treatment workshops offered by the hospital. The Marsden ran a workshop for parents of children who'd finished successful treatment. Although it was like being in a roomful of reverse lottery winners, I did come home from that day thinking, *I've heard enough about cancer now, I'm ready to move on.* (Wasn't quite as simple as that, though it was a useful stepping stone in the process.)

- Ask whether you and your child need a flu jab (non-live) and whether the treatment means that all the childhood immunisations need re-doing.

- Every time Cam had chemo, he was sent home with buckets of medication. We didn't need all of it as we already had ample at home. It can only be reused if it doesn't leave the hospital, so check what you have before you go.
- On the occasions where Cam ended up spending the night in hospital after a trip to A&E, we often had a long wait for the medication to arrive on the ward from the pharmacy so we could be discharged and go home. If it's approaching half past four and you're still waiting, start asking the nurses to chase it so that you don't end up spending another night in hospital because the pharmacy has closed.
- Although Steve and I both wanted to be there for every chemo session and every consultation, Cam hated the circus of us all blundering about the hospital with bags and coats and coffees. I was far too control-freaky to let Steve go without me, and he was generous enough to recognise that and let me get on with it. Ask your child what they prefer and try to respect that without taking it personally.

CHAPTER FIVE

Pat

Night of No Return

8–10 September 2017

I find myself awake at 3 a.m. This happens sometimes when Jan is away and I sleep more lightly. Caragh, our dog, stirs by my feet as I roll over. I hear a thud from the attic, Dom's room. Driven by an instinct so deep I can't ignore it (if you've felt it you know what I mean and if you haven't you probably won't believe it exists), I get up to check it out.

My nerves are jangling as I climb the attic stairs. The first thing I see is an empty bed, then Dom in the bathroom doorway. He pukes and I step back from the mess, more alert by the second. Is it food poisoning? Appendicitis? He pushes me away.

'Leave me alone, Mum.'

He pushes me again, more forcefully this time.

'Fuck off, Mum.'

A pit of dread begins to develop in my gut as he staggers around. Is he drunk? Biting back anger, I try to coax him onto the bed and as I do, tread on something with my bare foot. The crunch of plastic. It's then that I spot the empty pill packets all over the floor. Then the red and white label of a cheap vodka bottle. The scene takes shape very very slowly.

'What have you taken? Have you taken drugs, Dom? I need to know.'

Now I find myself in teacher mode – my emergency first aid training kicking in. I am totally focused on working out what is wrong and keeping Dom alive. But while my body might be running on instinct, my mind is on the ceiling watching events unfurl, numb and refusing to see that this is real, that this is happening to me.

Dom has collapsed onto the bed and his speech is muddled. He pulls the duvet over his head, curled up with his childhood cuddly toy, Doggie, in his arms. 'Come on, Dom, talk to me,' I shake his shoulders fiercely and, even at this point, am not sure what I am dealing with. Then I see it. Written in biro, in capital letters above his bed:

I LOVE YOU… NOT RESPONSIBLE… AT PEACE

Dom has taken an overdose. I see the thought in the same big capital letters. I make a snap decision and risk leaving him, running downstairs to get my phone. My hands are shaking and I have to focus all my concentration on dialling 999. My voice is breathy and I can feel the sweat in my armpits as I am talking to the emergency services while rushing back upstairs to Dom. They ask me if he is responsive and I try to move him but he won't budge. More than anything I want him to speak and open his eyes. To be alive. The kind voice says that she will stay on the line until the ambulance comes. While we wait, she takes some details and asks me to keep him moving or talking. I manage to shift him onto his side but other than that he makes no response and his breathing is laboured.

I try shaking his shoulder again then in desperation slap his face to stir him. He punches me hard in the shoulder, knocking me backwards, but the pain doesn't register. I recover my balance and push the shock down. At least he is responding. But he is strong and I wrestle back the fear of being hurt myself. I slap him again, harder than the first time, begging him to stay awake, terrified that he will die before the ambulance comes.

Even in this moment, my mind is efficient, coldly racing forward to what has to be done to leave the house. I am in my dressing gown and need clothes but Dom is slumped and I dare not leave him. Instead, I wait by his side, with the phone as my lifeline for what seems like hours. Where is the ambulance? The muscles in my arms are shaking continuously as I stroke his cheek and brush the golden hair from his forehead gently, whispering, 'Don't die, Dom. I love you. Please don't die.'

At last, the doorbell blares and I jump up. Taking the stairs as fast as I can, I fumble with the door, cursing our triple locks. The dog is barking fiercely by my side so I hurry her into the kitchen before I let them in. I have literally never been so glad to see another human being and could kiss them in gratitude. They enter, all professional in their green uniforms and completely calm. Unfortunately, the expressions on their faces do not shift my fear one single inch as they assess Dom. I'm not sure why I need their permission to chuck clothes on but I do and then, leaving him in their care, I rush to grab my purse to take it with me to the hospital.

I cannot bear to watch as they struggle to manhandle Dom out of the house, me trying to get out of their way and repeating *thank you* and *sorry* all the way to the door. I am so ashamed of what we have come to – it's as if my whole life is being judged under the harshest of lights.

As we hit the chilly night air, I quietly lock up the house, leaving a key under the mat for a friend to sort the dog out later. The streets are empty. There is no sound beyond the engine of the ambulance. The jarring blue light makes my pulse throb in my forehead. I hold Dom's hand and search fruitlessly for reassurance on the faces of the paramedics.

As we head to the hospital, I phone Jan, who is in Newcastle for work. He fumbles to answer and I tell him what's happened. I can see the paramedic has assumed that we are separated and it upsets me that I never find time to tell him this is not the case – I'm not even sure why it matters but it does – the judgement of our parenting and family that comes with the package of a suicide attempt. Knowing he is stranded without a car, I ask Jan when he can get here and we discuss trains and taxis. He wants to know if Dom will be okay so I ask the paramedic, holding the phone so Jan can hear. We don't get the straight yes that we want and instead the paramedic just explains that Dom will be assessed at the hospital. As the ambulance sways around the corners, I think about calling Greg, Dom's big brother, who has just gone back for his second year at Cornwall College, but I don't know what I would say to him and he can't do anything so I leave it for another time. I never let go of Dom's hand as we sway through the streets, I tell him it will all be alright, even though it's a parenting lie: the truth is I have no idea.

When the ambulance pulls up at the hospital, the medics go into the flurry of a well-rehearsed transfer from ambulance to A&E. The nurses and doctors move about with focus but their light chatter at the check-in desk seems like an assault on me personally. How can they when my son is here like this? I contain the anger that flares within me, realising that I need them on my side. Dom is aggressive and I am desperate. Even in these circumstances I find myself worrying about manners and what they will think of us.

One of them asks me to repeat the details again. I try to sound matter of fact about the forty paracetamol, the bottle of vodka and maybe a half bottle of gin. They write it down with no comments except that blood tests will be needed. They put him on a trolley, wheel us into a side room, close the curtain and leave.

After a few minutes with me sitting in the chair still holding Dom's hand helplessly, he starts to rant and tries to get off the bed.

'Let me die, Mum,' he yells.

'I can't do that. I love you and I want you to stay with us,' I plead.

'I love you but please let me die. LET ME DIE. I WANT TO DIE… Can I have a drink of water? I want Doggie.' I close off all my senses and bring him water from the sink by the bed. Doggie is at home. Dom takes a sip and falls back on the pillow, eyes closed. I watch his chest rise and fall. The tightness in my own chest is suffocating me but I dare not start to feel or think for fear of falling apart completely. The paramedic who carried Dom from the house arrives with a clipboard and asks if I can go with him to fill in the form.

We sit side by side in a forlorn waiting room in earshot of Dom as he takes all the relevant information down. Their questions are not even close to the ones I want answers to.

Dominic Patrick Sowa.

Seventeen years old.

1 June.

My Millennium baby, full of promise. I have a clear picture of driving to the very same hospital in the bluest dawn. The air spangled with energy and hope.

No, this is the first time.

The paramedic talks to me about his own four children and the difficulties of being a parent. An act of compassion from a stranger which makes me feel a bit less alone and not quite so much of a failure as a mother.

And now we sit and wait. Dom and I alone in our sparse cubicle. The sounds of other life-changing events all around us. An elderly gentleman with a suspected heart attack next door. A drunk man venting his frustrations on the staff, swearing and ranting. They shush him and steer him back to his bed. Quiet settles around us again. Dom is snoring, ghost white with grey lips and a cold, clammy hand in mine.

A nurse pops her face around the curtain to see how Dom is, and, smiling, offers me a cup of tea and brings it with a hug. It is this physical act that does it. For the first time I begin to cry, unable to stop. I fold over with the pain, my head on my knees, hugging myself. How has it come to this? What have we done wrong? Why weren't we able to stop it? Why didn't Dom tell us? What is wrong with us?

A doctor comes to see Dom. Frankly, I don't want to hand my precious son over to someone who looks so young but there's no alternative. He explains some complex information about when the blood tests can be taken. I try hard to take it in but there is not much space left in my tired and frightened brain. He says that we will have to wait four hours from when Dom took the tablets so nothing can be done until 7 a.m. My vision blurs and I cannot swallow. I start to panic – it feels unbearable to be able to do so little. 'Wait and see' does not seem like much of a plan to me.

The doctor asks if I have any questions. The only one I can come up with is 'Would you be happy with this treatment plan if it was your child?' He looks at me for a long moment and then says that he would. This is the sum total of my ability to control what is happening.

After three hours in A&E, Dom is found a space in a separate room on an adult ward. As he rolls onto the bed, he looks at me briefly with glazed eyes. I kiss his cheek and tell him I love him and just hope that he can hear me. I can't believe I am sitting there, not knowing if he is going to live through the next twenty-four hours. I cannot actually imagine that he will die. I love him too much for that to happen, surely?

Jan and I exchange texts. There are no taxis to be found so he is catching the first train out of Newcastle. I feel my jaw unclench a little knowing that he will soon be here alongside me.

The nurse brings me a blanket and a pillow so I kick my shoes off and make a nest on the chair beside Dom. I allow myself to close my eyes although I keep a hand on the back of his wrist.

My thoughts turn over incessantly as my shock unravels a little. I try to digest what has happened. How have we got here? Dom was in such good form over the summer. We had a fantastic holiday, the four of us, and we thought we were through the worst. Only twelve months earlier he had started a new school for sixth form ('Best year ever, Mum') and we thought the bullying he'd endured at secondary school was behind us. He'd been on happy visits to university open days with Jan. I'd let my guard down and now I am looking back at the past with altogether different eyes.

I drift back to last night. We were in the kitchen. My baby Dom now towers over me and I can see myself standing on tiptoe to reach upwards for a hug before he went to bed. I can still feel the feebleness of his squeeze in response. He's normally a great hugger but I'd put it down to tiredness from the start of term. It was much more deadly than that.

The clink of the breakfast trolley outside the door wakes me from a jagged sleep. I turn my neck side to side listening to the crick inside my head as I unravel myself from the thin blankets. Seconds later my Mother Alert button pings back on.

The light is soft in the room and I can hear Dom breathing steadily, see the white bed cover rising and falling in the rhythm of deep sleep. I gaze at his translucent skin, his blond hair, his long artistic fingers. He is six feet and one inch in his bare feet, his voice is deep and rich, and yet he still wants Doggie with him at bedtime. My beautiful man-boy.

Sitting here, this new-life morning, I have never felt so alone in my love for Dom. It swamps me and I am not sure I am grown up enough for the task of keeping him alive. The scale of this job, which I feel completely unequipped to handle, bears down on me with such intensity that for a moment my throat closes over. Placing my hands on the arms of the chair, I steady myself. Where there's life, there's hope and my job (at the very least) is not to add to the drama. But still, not for the first time since my dad died, I wish he would walk through the door and take over.

As before, it's the kindness of the lady who brings me tea that nearly undoes me.

I whisper a 'thank you' and Dom stirs in the bed, moans and pulls the blanket over his head. The tea lady and I exchange glances and she mimes a cup and saucer and points at Dom. I give her a thumbs up and she places a cup by his bedside. 'Here you are. This'll do the trick.' If only it were that simple. I mean, don't get me wrong, I know the NHS would stop functioning without tea but there are limits to its powers.

In the silence, as Dom stays hidden under the blanket, I concoct an email to school. I'm due to be taking assembly this morning and as the headteacher, I need to let them know that I will not be in. I say that I have a stomach bug, apologise and hit send. It doesn't feel great to lie but I am not ready to share events yet.

Shortly after, a trainee doctor arrives to take a blood test and fails after several wince-inducing attempts. In a voice as tight as cheese wire I request that he kindly fetch someone else to find the vein. I'm aware that I must seem like one of those thin-lipped, lemon-faced middle-aged women I always swore I wouldn't become, but it's my job to get things right for Dom. The doctor's eyes apologise and he sidles to the door in rapid retreat. Suffice to say, I do not see him again. Dom curls under the covers without a word.

When Jan finally arrives, there is no space in my feelings pot to think about how hideous it must have been for him to travel, not knowing if his child would be alive when he got here. Instead, having been the one holding the fort I become irrationally frosty. We are awkward in the space and the room suddenly seems even smaller. We hold each other but there is little comfort in the embrace. Neither of us has the strength to do anything other than keep ourselves together for Dom.

There is no privacy in the room so I offer to get coffee and leave Dom and Jan together. The hospital is busy and, invisible, I walk past patients, relatives and staff, the waft of medicine, fear, hope and cleaning fluid soaking into my pores. I'm playing a game in my head as I look at the faces of the passers-by and try to guess by looking into their eyes why they are here: tragedy, routine check, duty visit? Amid the hum of the hospital, I watch two nurses talking; one of them laughs and the other rolls her eyes before walking away. *Lucky them*, I think, *enjoying their casual everydayness, untouched by the shit that has hit my personal fan.*

I return to the new, unrecognisable and terrifying world I live in, contained in four walls with three cups of coffee, a newspaper and a pack of cards. It's not exactly an SAS survival kit list from which to build a 'new normal' but it's the best I can do.

Saturday 9 September

Dom asks for colouring books and pencils to pass the time and Jan leaps into hunter-gatherer mode and heads off to town. From my bedside chair, I try to stay quiet and let Dom lead the way. For someone who prides herself on being good in a crisis, I am totally out of my depth. I am torn between my determination to keep Dom alive and the dread of doing the wrong thing and making it worse. I have no idea whether to speak, what to say if I do or whether I should just endure the silence.

In the end, the risk of him thinking I don't care overrides everything else and I reach for him. He gives my hand a squeeze and my heart squeezes back. We sit, holding hands, looking at the concrete courtyard, the autumn shadows and golden trees adding a touch of beauty to the grey. 'I'm sorry,' he mumbles.

I want to take this pain away, I want to scream at the universe and ask it why my love alone is not enough. Instead, I give him a hug that I hope will tell him he has nothing to be sorry for. 'It's me who's sorry that you're hurting so much,' I say, wishing I could take him in my arms and rock him like a baby. Start again.

There is a tap on the door and Jan bustles in with colouring books. Dom drops my hand and immediately begins to flick through them. The only sound is the rhythmic scratching of the colouring pens and the rustle of the pages as Jan reads the paper. I check my phone.

The boredom and terror combo that comes with waiting for results settles over us until it is interrupted by the arrival of the consultant, who talks to Dom, barely acknowledging us. 'Well, you are physically in the clear.' My guts lurch. One hurdle crossed. 'Now we just need to sort your head out.' With that he leaves. Dom's face is bent back over the colouring book and is unreadable.

With his permission and reassurance that he is okay, I allow myself to go home for a shower. As I leave Dom for the first time in forty-eight hours, I have to remind myself that I am not the only one who is capable of looking after him. It's the same territorial feeling I had when he was newborn and relied on me for almost everything. The responsibility daunted me then and it comes back with full force. I cannot imagine how to persuade him to stay when he says he wants to die.

As I enter the house there is a chill atmosphere. The bed unmade, the curtains still closed. I open the place up and put some music on to take away the silence. Standing in the shower, the hot water barely registers and I turn the heat up until my skin is red. Even that does not thaw my brain.

With cardboard-flavoured toast to fortify me, I brace myself to go up to Dom's room. I can sense the room above me filled with blackness. My arms and legs tremble with the memory of finding him there (was that really only two nights ago?) but somehow I force myself to take each step. Barely breathing, I remind myself that it is only mess and he can't come home to it. I pretend that it is not me, not my family, not our mess and detach myself completely from the situation as I carry a bucket, rubber gloves, cloths and bin bags up the narrow stairs to the attic room.

I stand on the threshold and stare. The floor is covered in a sour jumble of clothes and vomit. The sheets and duvet are hanging off the bed, tangled from his thrashing about. School folders and a crumpled essay in his neat handwriting are hanging out of his rucksack, which is dumped as always by his desk. It's the only link to life before Dom took his overdose. The rest I am seeing through new eyes. This does not fit the image I have of my family and home.

I pull on the rubber gloves, and start to clean up, ramming everything into bags, picking out unsalvageable stuff to go straight to the tip and separating some clothes that I think I can rescue. His brand new checked trousers, worn with such style only a few days earlier, stop me in my tracks.

The whole scene reveals the sorry tale of Dom's state of mind. I see it in the harsh light of hindsight and wonder how on earth I could have missed the clues. But when you don't know what you're looking for, it's hard to spot. I keep my eyes down and firmly focus on what is in front of me because I know if I look up, I am going to see the writing on the wall, the message Dom left us.

Eventually I brace myself and sit on the edge of the bed. I pick up his sweatshirt and breathe in the smell of him. It takes me back to his daily mumbled 'morning' and hug, the brush of his smooth cheek on mine. I can see him making pancakes in his dressing gown, singing to himself, offering me one. I look at the Farrow & Ball wall (really – who cares now?). The biro scars out the words. I make myself read them again, imagine how desperate my little boy must have been. *I love you. You are not responsible in any way. I am at peace.* Finally, slow tears build to heaving sobs.

Eventually, they run dry and I sit, calmer now, but exhausted. The cat rubs against my legs and demands attention. I give her a head-rub and go back to cramming stuff into black bags. *Let's hope we can tidy up the emotional mess as easily*, I think, dragging the bags downstairs and dumping them one by one into the bin with grim determination.

Saturday 9 September, 16.45
Hello Fish

So I guess when troubles come they come not as single spies but whole battalions… I'm sorry to have to let you know that Dom is also very poorly: he has taken an overdose this week and is very luckily still with us but we face an as yet unknown future of mental health care and we may have a long road ahead.

We are writing not to add to your burden given the recent news for Cami but wanted to let you know so that you understand why we have gone quiet. We are thinking about you all and will share cannula stories one day…

I can imagine that it would make you really cross to hear this when you have Cameron fighting something he has not 'brought on himself' but for Dom his mental disease is just as deadly and not in his control. He is facing an invisible but deadly illness too.

Jan and I are reeling. No plans yet. Please think of us all.

Saturday 9 September, 18.31
Oh Patti

You poor poor things. And of course, we don't think for one moment that he has brought this on himself – as you say, it's a different type of disease and no less deadly for the absence of chemo shit. It doesn't make us cross, it makes us deeply sad. I am so so sorry to hear this, darling. What awful times, I bet you are reeling.

I hope we can support you the way you have supported us. After a drama-filled fortnight, Cami came out of hospital on Weds but he's back at school and our clouds have abated for the time being. We now have room and time for other people. Tell us when you are ready to talk, but in the meantime, we are all sending so much love and strength to you all.

Sunday 10 September

'Dom says that he did mean to die but is remorseful now and is glad that he is here.' The words roll over me as I sit in a bleak side room at the hospital. Jan and I have our coats on, perching on visitors' chairs, as if we would like to scarper at the first available opportunity. The two women from Child and Adolescent Mental Health Services (CAMHS) are sitting together on the regulation NHS bed.

My head is boiling that these total strangers dare to mediate my relationship with my son and think they have the right to tell me how he feels. I am being handed off, my role stripped away. At seventeen, Dom can tell them he doesn't want us involved, they explain. I freeze at the idea. I am stricken with shame that my parenting is so poor that my son has ended up feeling that it's better not to be here. The only thing I can cling on to is that he doesn't blame me, us. But what if he does? What if he tells them he doesn't want to come home and never wants to talk to us again?

My brain leaps from fear to fear so fast that I have him living on the streets, peddling drugs or being sexually exploited in only three mental moves. The outrageous sense of helplessness means I can barely take in what she is saying… 'Wants to come home… happy to have you involved in his care…' These words slowly register and I realise that we have avoided catastrophe. Passed an invisible test. DOM LOVES US. HE WANTS TO COME HOME.

Desperate now to get him away from all of this, we ask if we can all leave and they say yes. We accept the responsibility for his care and the weight of it settles on our shoulders as they explain the new rules and safety plan. Effectively we are on suicide watch with the rather unhelpful advice that 'if he is determined there is a limit to what you will be able to do'. That, a hand-written phone number for the crisis line (only open until 10 p.m.), and an instruction to put away all the medicines is the sum total of the support information we are given to keep our son alive. Jan and I look at each other and exchange tiny nods as the CAMHS team look on.

Pat's beginners' guide to mental health:
Lessons learned the hard way

Please be aware that this is a non-exhaustive list that barely skims the surface of a very complex subject and is only based on my personal experience.

- We all have mental health and most of the time we keep it on an even keel but sometimes we need expert help. It doesn't mean we're weak. We wouldn't expect a broken ankle to recover without going to the hospital, and mental ill-health needs the same straightforward approach.
- Love alone is not enough: knowledge and skills are also needed to support someone with a mental health condition.
- Mental health services are well meaning, mainly dedicated but often completely overstretched. Do not underestimate the possible impact of this.
- Now I would ask what the qualifications are of the person looking after me or a loved one. I'd also want to know how many other people they are seeing (fifty clients a week, an hour each is not in my view a manageable workload).
- Cognitive behavioural therapy (CBT) is currently the default setting for treatment on the NHS but it is not necessarily enough for a suicidal crisis. Ask about the specific support and pathways (the NHS term for 'plan') for suicidal crisis in your NHS mental health trust.
- Press to know if professionals are trained specifically in a recognised suicide prevention approach (for example, Applied Suicide Intervention Skills Training – ASIST).

- Find out about alternative approaches such as eye movement desensitisation and reprocessing (EMDR), if you can afford to consider the private route.
- Learn about symptoms and persist in getting assessment and help. Rather than 'hoping for the best' or that something will sort itself out, get early help before problems take root.
- It is important to ask about how suicide risk is assessed as it varies widely between NHS trusts. Best practice would include a safety plan developed with the person at risk and shared with trusted others.
- Ask directly if you will be told if they are concerned that your child is at risk. Over the age of sixteen, your child has to give permission for you to be informed. However, if it is to save a life, you should expect to be told unless there are specific circumstances.
- Ask for support as a family. It's hard to admit you need it but you would not expect to know how to manage diabetes without some training. Being a teacher, I am trained to look calm on the outside but my inside did not match. Professionals make assumptions (they're human too) so now I would be much more direct in explaining how at a loss I was, how frightened.
- If you have a friend in hospital for mental health, visit, message, send a 'thinking of you' card – treat it as you would a physical illness. Remember it's not their fault or a character flaw, and it's not catching.
- Be very specific about the behaviours that you are seeing that worry you and put it in writing to share with the professionals looking after your child. For example, Dom was not speaking and was scuttling off to his room at every opportunity but I was told that *Sometimes silence is a good thing.'* It would have been more helpful if I had written

down how many hours he was locked away and to describe his frozen, folded-in body language.

- Use direct language. Even professionals use euphemisms such as 'We are worried about…' And Dom's word for how he was feeling was 'sad'. Ask what they actually mean. It's okay to ask, *'Do you mean they/you are feeling suicidal?'*

CHAPTER SIX

Pat

Four Walls and Fumbling for a Future

Week of 11 September 2017

<u>Monday 11 September</u>

Pat to Kerry
Hi Fish

Very up and down today. I'm signed off work for this week and maybe next while CAMHS put support in place. Hunkered down at home with Dom who is 'in my care' and very difficult to both reach and read. Aaargh. But Jan and I did manage a short laugh this morning. Hope you guys are okay. Will call/let you know when I have some space as would love to chat.

Kerry to Pat
You poor bugger Patti,

Cam shut down for a while too. I think they have to process what has/is happening. It feels very isolating. Short laugh! Any laugh is good. Don't want to stalk you

but don't want you to feel alone. You are very much in our
thoughts. xxxx

My mind circles around the turns in the road, from the almost imperceptible decisions to the momentous ones that have brought us to this precipice. The hours stretch ahead bleakly. I'm definitely not on holiday but I'm not at work either, so what am I?

I'm having to keep a tight grip on practical stuff while the tectonic plates shift beneath my feet. I set about tidying the kitchen like a demented Dobby the house elf. Normally I would stick The Who on full blast but my ears are straining to hear every movement from upstairs.

I stay in the kitchen hoping that Dom will pass by. It seems better than hovering in the corner of whichever room he is in, waiting for him to become absorbed in a book or the television so I can peek at him. Not for the first time this week, I wish for a scanner like the one at the supermarket checkout but that can read moods and spot an oncoming suicidal crisis. Where are you when I need you, Bill Gates?

Dom appears. His throat is still too sore to swallow anything hard so he makes a smoothie in his beloved NutriBullet. *He is eating.* Taking his tobacco and lighter, exhausted by the burst of activity, he heads to his favourite spot in the garden. I stand in the lounge spying through the window. He pulls up his dressing gown hood boxer-style against the cold and, white-faced, he stares into the garden. He rolls a cig with careful precision and smokes it slowly, legs crossed and elegant. I hate him smoking but now is not the time.

In the afternoon, as the adrenaline of the last few days begins to retreat, unstoppable hot tears flow. I cannot get words to move from my mind to my lips. They are trapped by a huge lump of clotted emotions. Staring at the blotchy skin and wild-woman hair, I grimace at the mirror. This is not who I am. I'm a headteacher for goodness' sake. Someone others turn to for solutions to their own parenting problems. Yet here I am with no paddle in this particular canoe.

Tuesday 12 September

I don't want to be anywhere except looking after Dom, but I'm already going stir-crazy. Giving myself a mental B minus, I yank my rubber gloves on and go up to his room to scrub at the paintwork again but the biro message just won't shift. I give in. Instead, having put it off for as long as I dare, I head downstairs to call my elder son.

'Hi, Greg, how are you?' I wonder if he can hear my jittery stomach. I stick to the facts and try to sound reassuring. 'Let's hope so. He's in the right hands.' It's the closest I can get to an honest answer for the one question we all have.

Dropping this emotional atom bomb into Greg's life then putting the phone down and hoping for the best adds another layer of helpless responsibility.

Dom has been watching endless television. He has made it very clear that he does not want to talk about IT and when I mentioned this to CAMHS I received the reply that 'Sometimes silence is a good thing.' So I resist giving him the third degree and join him for an episode of *Come Dine With Me*, creating our own commentary and sharing our love of cooking.

Having had a few days in hiding, Dom now asks for his phone and iPad back. There is an edge of defiance in his voice, a tone that says he is willing to make a stand if necessary. I love that glimpse of fighting spirit but my mind races in a confusion of parenting and tech phobia. Dom is seventeen. He could walk out tomorrow and decide to go it alone and that is the one thing I just cannot risk at the moment. I 'lower the emotional temperature', in the new jargon of CAMHS, and hide my irritation as I watch Dom tap away, his agitation rising. As the replies come in his mood eases a little. His friends love him. I bank that as a good thing.

Dom takes himself off to sing at the piano behind the closed door of the dining room. He has played this piano and sung for hours at a time almost every day for the last ten years. Today it feels so precious that I creep up to the door and press my ear against it as he sings through his repertoire of ballads, his soaring voice full of the feelings that he cannot express in spoken words.

Wednesday 13 September

We have floundered into a new routine that hinges around cycles of visits from CAMHS, showers, singing, baking and TV for Dom while I try to read the runes of his mood to keep him safe without driving him up the wall. We have all agreed that Jan should go back to work and, to break the intensity, I pass time answering work emails. The intrusion of such once-important decisions backfires and my flittering brain can't find its aim to bat the problems away. Overwhelmed by the sense of responsibility for everyone else, I slap down the laptop lid.

It was my job as a mother to get him fledged (roots to grow, wings to fly and all that). Instead, here we are pulling back from the brink of suicide. All our trust is in the CAMHS treatment plan. If I followed my instincts I would take him away – whisk us off to Ireland and soak up nature with no Wi-Fi. But I also know that he might not want that and I dare not take him away from the lifeline of support.

Pat to Kerry
Hi Fish
   Dom has daily appointments with the Crisis Team then one with the psychiatrist coming up to try to work

out what's going on, then a medication/therapy plan. It's eerily parallel to your experience with Cameron, yet entirely different. GoCompare a serious mental illness with a serious physical one! Bloody stressful looking after him. Caught him reading Marilyn Monroe's autopsy results yesterday and he was flat already so that was enough to give me the full jitters. Ended up back with the Crisis Team by 5 p.m. with him telling me I was babying him. I'm being very grown up in front of him and have not admitted the shameful truth of how helpless I feel to anyone except you and one other friend. No idea quite what happens with school. But I can't imagine prowling around the house if he goes back. All still one day at a time. How's Cam at school this week? And is Michaela okay?

Big love xxxx

Every trip to CAMHS is a mini-break for me because they are in charge. But God, it's grim. Brown tired carpets, peeling paint, harassed-looking staff and the icing on the cake: all our fellow travellers with the same drawn faces, keeping their eyes to themselves. Silence reigns as, without exception, the teens flick past images that suck them into a different universe. Numbing out? From where I am sitting it sounds quite appealing.

I join Dom for the first part of the meeting with the psychiatrist and he shuffles in the chair next to me. I am given a chance to sum up three years of extreme anxiety (both his and ours). It becomes obvious as I dance on eggshells that this is not going to work. I'm invited to leave and agree, hoping that Dom is able to tell them what's going on. I one hundred per cent genuinely don't care if I'm not needed (well, maybe ninety-nine) but I'm terrified they won't realise how serious it is. And, above all, the protective mother bear is not sure that Dom will find his voice.

Thursday 14 September

At another appointment (is it Thursday?), Dom and I sit side by side across a table from the Crisis Team manager as I tell our story – his story. I feel an enormous pressure to remember everything in the allocated hour and also to give Dom airtime. I can't squash it all in and hand over the notes that Jan and I have made so they have everything. I can't help wondering if I may as well have stuffed them into a bottle and thrown them into the ocean, but it's our only hope.

As I speak about Dom's life, some of the tension inside loosens and it seems to have lifted Dom too because he whistles as we get home. I press my fears for the future to the back of my mind and we settle in to watch *Keeping Up with the Kardashians*. From a standing start it has become my specialist subject this week as I try my best to get alongside Dom.

The doorbell interrupts us and I practically fall into the entire contents of the ready meal shop, COOK, on the porch. I guess who it's from before I even read the card. Dragging the box into the house, I reach for my phone:

Pat to Kerry
Thank you thank you thank you Fish. I can't get out so food is the perfect gift. Life is very tense. Dom thinks I'm over-reacting but even though I'm terrified we will lose him, there's a huge part of me that wants to yell 'It's not just your feelings that count!' Don't tell anyone I said that. It's so selfish of me.

Squeezing as many boxes as possible into the freezer becomes an all-consuming task, which I am absolutely determined to achieve but still fail at. Defeated, I rant at the fridge, which stands immovable and rattle off instructions for Jan to spread the spare meals throughout the freezers of Yorkshire.

I sit at the kitchen table. The door is ajar and every nerve is on full alert to the slightest shift in atmosphere. With a long sigh, I flip open the laptop; it's time to update our closest friends and family. What a gloomy round robin I am sending, knowing that I am spreading sorrow instead of sharing joy. It opens the scars left by losing Mum and Dad not so long ago. There is a huge part of me that would prefer to leave everyone out of it – to battle on alone – and it takes a monumental effort to work my way through the email list. Mental note: make more contact when there is good news. Also, please can someone tell me why family politics still matter? The pecking order of calls and emails takes a good five minutes to navigate.

There are so many questions, both spoken and left unsaid: 'What's wrong with him? With you?' 'Is it drugs?' 'Why?' That's before anyone even homes in on the stigma of a suicide attempt: 'How can he do that when he has everything to live for?' 'He'll be alright.' 'It's a cry for help.' These comments cut me with their lack of understanding but I know they are well meant and wrapped in loving support. They are things I have thought myself in the darkest hours. So I clench my teeth and absorb the shame, the shock and the sadness. I start to form a different view on mental illness. It is as deadly as physical illness, an invisible disease curled inside but not created by Dom. I have a fierce instinct to shelter my son from judgement. I reassure everyone that we are coping and that we will keep in touch, when all I really want to do is lock the door and hide until it all goes away.

Friday 15 September

In less than a week we have a new regime. The days before are lost to me. Each morning the anxiety kicks in deep in my bones. It reminds me of waking before baby Dom needed feeding to catch him before he cried. I count my blessings that we still have life and later, once I have heard Dom singing in the shower, my breath evens out and my throat unclenches a little more.

This new life is a lesson in living one moment at a time. I pretend that Dom is recovering from appendicitis; it helps me see his exhaustion and respond with patience to the dressing gown and duvet routine as he nests on the sofa. I wish it was something concrete like that – something that the NHS has a plan for which involves specialists and a clear route. Something that doesn't make the experts look worried. Even Cameron, whose cancer is rare, is having his chemotherapy at the world-leading Royal Marsden and being offered reflexology massage to boot. The contrast couldn't be greater for Dom, who is waiting for a counsellor to find a slot for a one-to-one appointment.

Each day I try to find a way to nudge him outdoors without being a nag. Although he's ill, he still has a stubborn streak; if he spots what I am doing he resists, though we both know he enjoys it once he gets out. I suggest town but for Dom this is an absolute no-go area for fear of bumping into someone. And I really know how he feels.

Remembering his love of nature when he was younger, I ask him if he will come to the garden centre with me and he agrees. We walk through the warm bright shed filled with vases and garden furniture and examine all the things you don't need but would really like to have. I am pleased with my ingenuity for thinking of this place – we barely see anyone and when we do it is clear that we lower the average age by a couple of decades. We spend a long time looking at bird feeders, discussing the merits of each type and where we might put one. I am itching to fulfil his every need and find magic 'cheering up' cures, so we buy the biggest one we can fit in the car and stuff the boot full of sunflower seeds, robin mix (who knew?), peanuts and fat balls.

Dom wanders to the bulbs and is quickly engrossed. I'm still in buying mode and put a basket in his hand, encouraging him to pick as many as he likes while I chirp on self-consciously about the cycle of the seasons.

We gather purple and white crocuses, deep red tulips, and spring yellow daffodil bulbs. Each carefully labelled in paper bags as Dom plans meticulously, weighing each decision, taking forever to make his mind up. I am in no rush to finish and anyway, I admire the artist in him, knowing I could never be so precise.

The optimist inside me fast forwards to spring. Together we will plant these in the garden and enjoy waiting until they emerge in all their glory after a long dark winter.

CHAPTER SEVEN

Pat

Navigating Our New Normal

Week of 14 September 2017

Just days after Dom could not see how to stay on this planet, we face a meeting to discuss a return to school plan. Jan and I have talked ourselves to a standstill over this decision (which isn't even ours to make).

So here we are, me perched on a sofa opposite a hunched Dom popping his knuckles one by one. At least he has changed out of his grey trackies into jeans for the occasion. He is flanked by CAMHS and the head of sixth form. I didn't sit next to Dom for fear of crowding him but now he looks vulnerable, shrinking into the sofa as if he wants to merge with it, no eye contact with anyone and the centre of attention. The adults weave a plan around him that sounds sensible – edging towards a return to normal. My thinking is slow under the pressure to get it right. It all relies on him being able to share how he is feeling; it seems so shaky when I did not spot how desperate he was last week and he didn't tell me. Dom and I have chatted it all over so I make myself let him take the final decision. CAMHS are confident that back to normal is the right strategy so I swallow my doubts and we agree the end of next week, just before the weekend, to get him in the swing.

Dom has developed a pattern to manage his agitation, which increases as we near the allotted time for the appointments that drive our days: breakfast smoothie concoction, TV, shower, sing, dry hair. He picks out his depression clothes: darkest grey sweatshirt and tracksuit bottoms. It shocks me each day how little attention he is paying to his appearance when normally he is so immaculate. I point him towards the clean clothes in the airing cupboard but he mumbles that these are the only comfortable things he has. I keep the peace.

It has apparently been decided that the focus of treatment is social anxiety. It is not remotely clear to me how this decision has been made. And this compounds my worries about what Dom is actually telling the bewildering trail of professionals he is meeting on a daily basis. How can it be right that I am not allowed to know what is going on? How am I meant to keep him safe when I am in the dark? Would these professionals stand for it if it was their own child?

It's almost unbelievable that I was blithely fretting about when to nudge Dom into completing his UCAS form so he could apply to university. I wonder if I'm the only one who completely missed the massive tyre-bursting pothole in their child's life-plan?

CAMHS have suggested things to help: a worry tin and a soothe bag. Dom politely agrees to give them a try, receiving a smile of approval from the counselling team. Having seen them out, he promptly switches off his impeccable manners, telling me in no uncertain terms that he thinks it's a waste of time. Biting back my own anger, I cajole him into trying it out by appealing to the shopper in him. We engineer the timing of a trip to town to minimise the chance of a social encounter and stock up on his soothe bag shopping list: candles, bath bombs, reading books, art pads, pens and pencils of all descriptions. He smiles not quite to the eyes as I hand it over to him. There is nothing I would not buy (or indeed sell) if it might soothe Dom's soul but this haul seems pitiful.

I have less luck with the worry tin, which succeeds only in adding more to my own already full-to-busting bucket of worry. He huffs and puffs, treating it like unwanted homework. Finally, job done, he takes the 'unfounded worries' and dumps them in the compost bin. The founded worries are in the tin, silently testing me. The only thing that stops me looking is the thought of what the hell I would do with the knowledge. That and the fear of being caught.

For the first time since my personal shit-fan saga exploded in all directions, I snatch a catch-up with my closest friends. At our first regular tea and therapy slot since Dom's overdose, I hear myself laugh and barely recognise it. Later, Jan and Dom join me for a pizza at ASK Italian. Nervous of hitting the wrong note, we start off on the safe territory of the menu. Dom chats freely this time and soon we're laughing together and the elephant in the room shrinks into the corner.

Knowing that Dom is due to go back to school next week has given a sense of urgency to the freedom we have left. We piece together a programme of life-affirming entertainment. A sort of homemade care plan intended to persuade Dom that it is worth being here.

Every trip has a surface level of calm and an undercurrent of emotional weather. Each thing has been carefully selected by Dom and reflects his passions: the art gallery at Salts Mill where he designs a bracelet for me to mark Jan's and my twenty-fifth wedding anniversary. A drive out to Sandsend reliving bucket-and-spade day trips. The sand wedges between our toes, and our fingers are sticky with ice cream, salt on our lips. Another day experimenting with his new watercolours and inks at Newby Hall where we paint in the rain. As the hours pass, we find our way back towards conversation and closeness by focusing on the concrete pleasures around us. Attempts at anything more probing result in Dom withdrawing into himself, eyes cloudy. Living has taken on a new intensity. Right now, he wants to be in my presence and I am grateful for that.

'How would you rate your mood today?' I tentatively ask. The black cloud above his head might as well be on the weather map.

'You're not a therapist,' he snaps and I bite back my retort. In the pause he mumbles, 'Minus three.' Now I wish I'd never asked. It is all very well CAMHS telling us to contact A&E if we are worried but on that basis I would be camping out there.

At home, we feel our way back through the little daily things: cooking, reading, watching TV together. These are genuine acts of love way more precious than any grand gestures. In the calmer evenings, Dom perfects his scone recipe and I (and even Jan) gamely try to keep up with the Kardashians. As Dom heads off for bed with his phone in hand, I give myself a good talking to about how ridiculous it would be to rummage in the attic for a baby monitor to put in his bedroom.

Towards the end of the week, Dom ventures out for only the second time since his overdose. He is meeting his 'soul sister', Immie, who is off to university. It's a five-minute walk but it might as well be a stroll on the hard shoulder. For want of a better plan and to make it a lot harder to stalk him down the street, I am up to my neck in hot bathwater nursing a glass of wine and waiting for the knots in my nerves to unravel. It's not top of the list of healthy coping strategies but right now it's the only one I have.

I wake the next morning to a day full of appointments in preparation for Dom's return to school. He heads off to the barber for a haircut and I dare an inner smile at the milestone. I have to remind myself that if he is going back to school tomorrow then he can walk to town today. It seems as if we are in an awkward three-legged race as we navigate between his feisty independence, his desperate neediness and my sense of responsibility for him. Magnified by an illness I cannot see, the roller coaster of these teenage years has been turned into the biggest dipper in the dark.

I can only hold on and hope that we will laugh when we stagger off at the other end.

> Kerry to Pat
> *Very hard being off work. I still don't want to do all the drudgy jobs I thought I would do when I had time! But we've got to be there for our boys so no option really, is there? Big week this week with kidney function day tomorrow and chemo on Thursday. Hope all becoming a bit clearer at your end. Sending love to you all. xxxx*

> Pat to Kerry
> *Cleaned my front door for the first time in my life! Spent half an hour talking to Dom's school today and came back to find him under a black cloud, so as you say, no alternative (and I really know it's the right thing even though it's not easy). Hope the tests are really positive. Send my love to Cami too. Hope he's managed to fleece a few quid off everyone playing Twenty-ones. xxxx*

Dom is tetchy about going back to school so I am dancing around him trying to distract, discuss or deny in rotation. He reassures me he will check in with the teacher, and I cook his favourite veggie toad in the hole for dinner before he slinks off upstairs. Churning through the long list of possible catastrophes, I know there is no plan except to hope that it turns out alright. I wish love was enough.

CHAPTER EIGHT

Kerry

The Only Thing Worse than Pumping in Poison

14 September 2017

Kerry to Pat
Went to a UCAS meeting at school last night where I had to face lots of people for the first time doing that 'You need to read my friend with bowel cancer's blog', 'He needs to eat warty humpback toad' plus plenty of 'I'm sure he'll be fine' and that bloody head tilt! But at least now he's back at school, I no longer have a warning siren going off in my head every five minutes.

Pat to Kerry
Oh my God, the head tilt! Glad to hear the alarms eventually grow quieter. Don't think I'm at that point yet.

Cam's hair is falling out and he's asked me to shave his head. I buy clippers, pretend that it's a fashion statement, and squirrel away a lock in my memory box next to the one from his first ever haircut. He stands in front of the mirror and laughs at his reflection. While I go upstairs to sob where he can't see me, he makes a joke of it all on Instagram and changes his avatar to a bald bloke cartoon. He comes home from school desperate to recount the story about the teacher who raised his eyebrows and said, 'Wow! That's an extreme haircut.' Cam didn't enlighten him but someone clearly did as the teacher then called him out of a lesson to apologise. We all kill ourselves laughing as Cam hams it up, imitating the teacher cringing and grovelling. Poor bloke.

At the weekend, some of Cam's friends are taking part in a run to raise funds for the Marsden. I love that they are doing that for him but still hold off asking for donations on Facebook. We're not quite ready to be the 'cancer family' yet. In fact, Cam feels a bit awkward about being there, the charity case with his bald head, and chooses not to come. I leave it up to him, trying to shake off decades of ingrained thinking around manners and 'the show must go on'. Actually, the boy with cancer should get to decide how he uses his time in case it's finite, but making the mental adjustment away from 'letting people down' is hard. I don't insist, but force myself to go even though I feel like putting a bag over my head so no one recognises me. I'm already sick of people patting me or assuming they can hug me. At the last minute, Cam comes with me. There's a Royal Marsden tent there and Cam and I head over to tell them how grateful we are for what they are doing for him. Halfway there, I know I'm not going to add value to the conversation as the sight of all the bibs with the names of people in whose *memory* the participants are running lodges a lump in my throat that refuses to budge. 'I can't do this, Cam,' I say and we do an about turn and watch the run instead.

We clap Cam's friends over the finish line. I take photos of them all together, Cam's grey pallor a contrast to their flushed faces and robust physiques. I start to cry and yet again, I have this sense of having to tidy up my emotions so I don't embarrass the people around me.

In the months that follow, social interactions follow a similar pattern. I can only be in a group setting when I'm at my most positive, usually when Cam has just had chemo, and I can make people laugh about the times at A&E when we've sat waiting for X-ray results dreading that there'll be some big fat tumour springing up somewhere else; the blood tests when they've turned Cam into a pincushion when they haven't been able to find a vein; the times Cam has sat having chemotherapy next to some poor kid puking up behind a curtain. Sadness one-to-one is just about acceptable as long as it doesn't go on too long; heartbreak in a group setting is too awkward for everyone.

But more pressing than how the hell we became a society that puts the onus on the person who's suffering to jolly everyone along is the need to keep Cam well enough to bounce from chemo to chemo every three weeks. I'm not a natural nurse but I have to inject Cam with Filgrastim to boost his neutrophils (blood cells that fight infection). I think it's safe to say I won't be retraining as a nurse if the book writing doesn't pan out, but I manage with patience and goodwill from Cam. Every week Cam has blood tests to check his levels and make sure he can cope with the chemo. He astounds me – every time so far, he shovels down a bucketful of tablets and gets up and goes to school as normal the following day. He hasn't yet missed a single day except for the actual treatment. And every time the chemo has been pumped in, a little bit of me relaxes, as though we've made it to a place of safety a few metres further up a sheer rock face. I make a chart to tick off all the tablets he has to have over the three weeks, wondering what percentage of patients die because their lives are too chaotic to master the complicated medication regime.

Disaster strikes. Despite my best efforts spraying all the door handles and light switches with antibacterial spray, Cam gets a cold and we end up in A&E. Blood tests show that his neutrophils are too low for chemo the following day. I leave Cam asleep in A&E at 3 a.m. I tuck a note into his headphones, telling him I love him and I'll be back first thing. I don't want Michaela to wake up again in a household where I'm not there. It's her GCSE year and although I personally couldn't care less about an A* in Maths when we're staring down the barrel of losing Cam, it's still important to her. I don't want her to get the impression it's only Cam who counts. She seems to be coping, taking it all in her stride, but maybe she just feels she can't claim any attention when Cam is so ill. I'm frightened to examine that thought too deeply in case I find another pit of guilt to fall into, without enough resources left to clamber out again.

Cam missing chemo unhinges me. I burst into tears in front of a good friend when I'm out with the dog but just walk off, leaving him standing there helplessly. I can't be comforted. There's not a single thing anyone in the world can say to me to alleviate my worry. All I can picture is the cancer stretching out octopus tentacles throughout his body, laughing as it unfurls at the unexpected freedom to spread and engulf. The next night I fly out of bed, convinced that I've heard terrorists with machine guns storm the house to shoot Cam dead. I run along the landing, flinging his door open and scaring him half to death. I'm frightened to go back to sleep in case the dream picks up where it left off.

The following day, Cam googles his cancer for the first time. He comes down to me, white-faced. 'Mum, I've just seen that I've got a sixty per cent chance of being alive in five years.' I've never googled anything. I can't risk knowing a single fact that might make me more worried than I am already, but I force myself to read what he has seen. Thankfully, there's a line at the bottom with some criteria that might boost the chances of living longer such as being young and catching the disease at an early stage. I convince him – but sadly not myself – that the gloomy statistic is skewed by older people who have other health problems and don't discover the cancer until much later. 'Do you think I'll die, Mum?'

I push down the huge swell of fear. I'm not a natural liar. And I don't know the answer anyway. I dig deep. 'No, I don't.' Even if it is a lie, there's plenty of time to be wretched later. We don't have to start right now.

CHAPTER NINE

Pat

First Day Back at School

22 September 2017

My hug is too tight as I remind Dom to text if he needs me. He pulls away, nodding, and I clock how tight his jaw is, the blue-black rings under his eyes, his pale skin. I fold my arms against me, fighting the instinct to pull him back into the house and to hell with school. He puts his left ear bud in, shucks his rucksack onto his shoulder and heads off. Thank God for the dog, who brings endless optimism and something to draw me out of myself. I press the volume key on my phone to full whack and put the vibrate and alert on for good measure. I move things from one place to another to kill the time. My stress levels shoot off the scale at the ringtone and I squeak out a 'Thank you for telling me' as I hear he is safely at school. Leaning my elbows on the worktop, tears flow and I push my palms to my eyes. And repeat.

Kerry to Pat
Bless you! Steve says wish we could transport between kitchens! We've had a SHIT week. Cam got a cold on Weds, which led to a night in A&E plus cancellation of chemo, which sent my stress levels off the scale. Currently sobbing into

wine on the grounds that with Cam on antibiotics, no reason (haha) to suspect that we'll have to rush to hospital though I don't think God was listening last time we made other plans! Cam obvs out with friends oblivious and joyful! How did Dom cope with school? We think of you so much and wish we could manically laugh together every evening. xxx

Pat to Kerry
The hardest part of this parenting lark is actually letting them live the life they want to live through all the shit they are going through and at the same time trying to stay sane ourselves… Hope Cam feels better soon and gets his next dose of chemo. A-levels and uni are looking a bit of a stretch for Dom at the moment – trying not to jump fences too early but the gap between where we are now and where we need to be for that feels huge…

Having been barricaded in the house, I venture out food shopping. Wrapped in a force field that separates me from everyone else, I have to dodge absolutely everyone who inhabits Planet Normal because I do not have words for any of this and panic is lurking in the wings in case someone expects me to be in headteacher mode. I pick off-piste shops and for a few minutes I pretend not to be me. I choose not to rain on the cashier's innocent instructions to 'have a nice day'.

As the week passes, the strain of being at school begins to show. Dom's moods swing from black to grey with the odd burst of weak sunshine. When a charm of goldfinches descends on the new bird feeder, I grab the good omen with both hands and when he and one of his besties giggle over baking in the kitchen, I chalk it up greedily.

CAMHS have done a disappearing act this week and my frustration at missed calls boils over one evening when, by 9.45 p.m., they still have not called to check in with him. I rant into my journal to avoid a public meltdown but it does nothing to ease my growing fears over the transition to adult care that looms come his eighteenth birthday. I'm already worrying about *that* hurdle.

Kerry to Pat
Poison is in! It really comes down to something when the happiest I've been in weeks is when I know Cam is brimful with a toxic cocktail… Managed school the following day and partied on over the weekend. Our issue now is that he's getting used to the world revolving around him, barely looking up from the phone to bark out some order for his mother to scurry off and do! I keep thinking about going back to work but then there's some drama and I can't even contemplate it. Topped off the week with the mother of all rows about what to do at Christmas. I don't want to be far from the hospital but everyone else doesn't want to be sitting staring at each other over the table on our own.

Pat to Kerry
I hear you on the work front – it's so hard to be everyone's skivvy, isn't it? Very brave of you to be talking about Christmas. I am anticipating tumbleweed at the table and seriously hope the four of us are still here to celebrate it. We do more toasts to absent friends these days than the people who are still here…

CHAPTER TEN

Pat

For Better or For Worse

7 October 2017

Teachers, mental health workers, friends and family – apparently everyone *except me* – feel very reassured that Dom is 'getting back to normal', which is proven by the fact that he is back at school. I, on the other hand, hate seeing his growing exhaustion at the effort of attending and am living with sick dread in my stomach. Life is semi-frozen with the fear of what might be.

A triumph of normality this week as halfway through building a desk, I have to trek back to IKEA to buy another £2.50 leg. Un-bloody-believable that I did not count properly. Who thought of a desk with FIVE legs?

Friends and relatives are texting and calling in their support. It's kind but I cannot find the words to tell them what this is like. The dark underbelly of life with our mentally ill child feels impossible to expose: it is Dom's story more than mine and the complex guilt around what has gone wrong means I don't know where to start. Better to pass it off with platitudes: 'He's having a difficult time at the moment.' 'I'm okay – parenting is never easy, is it?' 'Teenage years…' A wall of words to hide behind. Fish, my fellow traveller, and I have a dark and outrageous-to-the-outside-ear belly laugh on the phone.

> Pat to Kerry
> *Sooooo glad that we have each other. Massive help although I wouldn't wish it on you. Thank God we are going through similar things (you know what I mean).*

I'm still not sleeping and it's worse when Jan is away for work. I am restless, crumpling the sheets and thumping the pillows until, most nights, I creep in to check on Dom. It reminds me so much of listening in the dark when he was small that my heart hurts. 'Love you to Pluto and back a million times, Dom,' I whisper and return to my fitful non-rest.

It's Friday at last and there is one more hurdle before we can escape to our weekend in London. Dom is pacing the rooms, waiting for CAMHS to arrive. He becomes highly agitated but still no one shows up. After thirty minutes the phone rings. There has been a mix-up. We thought here, they thought there. I swallow a gut full of rage and although I can barely get the words out, we agree a new date.

We are off to meet Greg and celebrate our silver wedding. It will be the first time we've seen him since all this kicked off, although we have spoken regularly.

I love the train. This tin box which traps us in one place and where the only thing that can happen is a derailment or something else so random that it definitely is not my fault. Dom sleeps the entire journey. He looks so fragile I want to wrap him in blankets.

He perks up in London and I imagine him living there, being urban, cool and arty. Jan has done such a great job of adjusting our original plan (romantic getaway for two) that neither Dom nor Greg has realised.

Jan and I catch each other's eyes as we arrive at the theatre to see *An American in Paris* with Dom in tow. It's just around the corner from our first date. For better or worse. In sickness and in health. I have never given much thought to those vows over the years but we are drawing on them now. Testing their worth in the last few weeks – the toughest we have faced together. *Should have read the small print*, I think to myself.

The following evening, we are all dressed up for a celebration meal. Dom striking in his electric blue sweater, peroxide blond hair flicked back while Greg is equally eye-catching having just arrived from Cornwall rocking the surfer vibe. Jan is looking stylish in Italian cashmere and I feel old and knackered. Every day since OD Day is etched on my face and every scone I have eaten out of love for Dom is wrapped around my girth.

I put the face on and we raise a glass to our boys and to each other. Having both Greg and Dom in the nest, right here with us, is the greatest feeling. It's even more acute because Jan and I know how differently things could have turned out three weeks ago. I wonder how Greg is feeling about being here. He hates London so it's a huge act of love (or duty?) to come, without the challenge of adjusting to so much change since he last saw us, especially as he only went back to university a few weeks before. He and Dom had been getting on so well this year, so it must hurt.

Despite the ritual *Happy Anniversary* toast it's not easy to find satisfaction in twenty-five years of marriage when Dom's suicidal crisis seems like an epic failure on our part. After a long and painfully heated conversation, Jan and I have decided that we cannot be the ones who give Dom a drink. We fear that by doing this we are making life even more miserable for him but we hold the line, shooting glances at each other to check our resolve while he sulkily sips a glass of Coke.

We circle the conversation awkwardly, each trying to find our footing in this new scenario. We are all making it up as we go along and the strain of trying not to say the wrong thing makes it almost impossible to say anything at all.

Jan gamely tries a few openers. Football? No, not for Dom, who gazes off into the distance, shoulder turned to the group. The play last night? Good for Dom but Greg grimaces; was not there. The future? Don't even think about it. I heave an internal sigh of relief when the food arrives. The rich aroma of neutral territory is found in the mushrooms and tarragon and the atmosphere thaws as we compare notes. We all love Italian food – something to glue us together at last as we bring back memories of our holiday in Puglia just this summer.

Jan and Dom animatedly discuss the interior and lighting of the restaurant and Greg and I chip in only to be rebuffed cheerily by the two experts in the family. At the sound of laughter around the table I feel tears well up and push them away. Carpe diem.

CHAPTER ELEVEN

Kerry

Walk a Mile in My Shoes and Then We'll Talk

October 2017

Tuesday 17 October

Kerry to Pat
Very stressful week so far. Half-term and Cam out till two every night refusing to accept that it's not the best preparation for chemo on Thursday! Hope better your end?

Pat to Kerry
I cannot imagine how frustrating that must be with every ounce of your energy going into the chemo/stay alive plan. Must take huge control – I'd be sorely tempted to rant. Off to Cornwall to see Greg next week and genuinely looking forward to it. Starting to see the odd patch of blue sky behind the clouds.

Wednesday 18 October

Kerry to Pat
Have ranted! Finally got to bed at 3 a.m. on Monday night amid ferocious texting. I'm running on pure cortisol today, just trying to get Cam over the finish line for tomorrow

virus-free. Today is not a good day. Seeing Greg sounds wonderful and just what you need.

Pat to Kerry
Don't feel bad about ranting – they still need some boundaries and a bit of respect for the effort we are putting in. He will realise one day. (But don't wait standing up!)

In the weeks leading up to Cam's eighteenth birthday at the end of October, I want to celebrate all of his life, make sure he knows how much joy he's brought us, even if there's the heartache of losing him ahead. In fact, that's one of the huge shifts in thinking for me. I'd always thought it would be so painful to lose a child that you'd wish you'd never had them. Now I know that it's a privilege to hold their hands for as long as you get given. I am so grateful for the seventeen years I've had with my boy. I decide to make a huge photo album for his birthday. I think of it as *This Is Your Life*, then keep crying in case it becomes *This Is Your Far Too Short Life*.

I trawl through all the Bonusprints from the early years, loving all the funny faces, the blurred failure shots that now we'd simply delete on our phones. I start with the obligatory photo of me holding him in hospital, the boy I'd greeted with 'Welcome to the world', never imagining for one second that he might leave it before me. I add in all the photos common to hundreds of family albums, including him pushing his sister on a swing when she was a baby. It is ironic that they've only become really close in the last year, since Cam learned to drive. The commute to school has become fertile ground for swapping confidences that 'you mustn't tell Mum'.

I hope Michaela's managing. She seems to be ploughing forward, getting on with school, socialising, but who knows what effect all of this is having on her? She doesn't like me discussing it in front of her friends and shouted at me for blurting out that Cami had cancer to a mother at school who asked how I was in that 'just passing the time of day' way, then stood open-mouthed in a 'Fuck me, I didn't expect an honest answer and certainly not one like that' way. I don't blame Michaela for finding me embarrassing. I wish I could put on a face and smile and say everything is fine. But I can't and I don't know whether it ever will be again. Fifteen is too young to be dealing with this sort of shit. So is fifty-one, I'm finding.

I carry on, only able to do twenty-minute bursts of photo sorting before sadness gets the better of me. I stare at the picture of his primary class when he was about seven. An image of all those little children running around the playground with targets on their backs – 'This one will die of cancer', 'This one will die in a car crash', 'This one will get diabetes' – pushes into my mind.

I wish I could go back and do it all better, with more patience, more time, less interest in making sure he'd nailed the spelling of 'onomatopoeia' and more skiving off on sunny days to drive to Norfolk and jump the waves under those big open skies. I stare at the holiday photos, ashamed of how hard I found the early years when Steve and I fantasised about having a few days away on our own, with a lie-in beyond 6.30 a.m. In particular, I remember Cam, aged three, dragging me to sit on the outskirts of a hotel complex in Provence to watch a digger moving earth for hours at a time. And how I kept trying to get him to leave because I was bored. How differently I would have done it, had I known that the timer had been turned over, that the grains of sand were racing through, far, far more quickly than I'd ever imagined.

But the photos that stop me dead are the ones from the previous summer. We were in California after Cam's GCSEs. We're all there cycling around San Francisco, posing at Universal Studios without a care in the world, our biggest worry whether he might get a D in History. I can't compute that he was there with shiny hair, the ubiquitous baseball cap, making us laugh as we toasted marshmallows in Yosemite. And now he's approaching adulthood with less hair than the day he was born. Of all the scenarios I imagined when we put him into the car seat for the first time and the midwife waved him off from Bolton Hospital, saying, 'Have a nice life,' this wasn't one of them. I debate over putting in a picture of the four of us taken at a dinner a few weeks earlier. Will he want reminding of how he looks now? On balance, I decide it would be more offensive not to include it, a denial of where we are at, as though this bit of life is worth nothing at all. I hope those pictures of him with his round, steroid-filled face and bald head will just be a snapshot in time, sandwiched in between many Christmases and birthdays, maybe even his wedding in the future. It feels like tempting fate even thinking that far ahead.

Before Pat heads off to Cornwall, I call her to wish her a happy holiday. We spend half an hour laughing shamelessly about people's responses to our respective nightmares. I recount the story of an acquaintance who, first of all, had come at me like a lobster, all great waving arms and a dramatic, 'Oh how are youuuuu?' Then she proceeded to ask me whether the oncologist had talked to me about diet, followed by 'I've always made my kids blueberry smoothies every morning'. The main implication seemed to be that I, on the other hand, had been sending my kids to school clutching a can of pop and a packet of crisps so the cancer was somehow my fault, easily avoided if only I'd had a crackdown on dodging the Brussels sprouts. Sadly for her, I was actually the food tsar when my kids were young, quite the mother about town with the oatcakes and organic apricots after swimming lessons and homemade avocado ice cream (which clearly they took one look at and rejected resoundingly, taking the opportunity at every birthday party to circle cakes and crisps like sharks around a bleeding body). I ranted on: 'And a fat lot of good that did me so now we're mainlining bloody Percy Pigs!'

In the same week, someone I bumped into asked how Cam was getting on then said, 'He'll never get travel insurance again, you know.'

I did manage to say, 'Well, on the bright side, that might not be a problem because he might not live long enough to need it,' before stomping off, wondering what the hell was going through his head when he let those words make contact with the air. (To be fair though, in the months that followed, it became clear that many people blundered out with seemingly thoughtless comments because they panicked and felt they had to say something.)

Pat counters with her own versions – 'What he needs is some mindful colouring books.' 'It's just a cry for help.' I put the phone down feeling so much better. There is at least one person in the world who really gets it.

Thursday 19 October

Pat to Kerry
Hi Fish, Thinking of you all today. Hope chemo goes smoothly. Xx

Kerry to Pat
Already been hideous. Can't get cannula in because veins are shot from overuse. Cam had a meltdown, which set me off. May these be our WORST BLOODY DAYS.

Pat to Kerry
Oh shit! Surely there must be an easier way than vein hunting!

Kerry to Pat
All calm now. Mythological vein discovered. Poison flooding in. How long until we can go out and get absolutely trollied together?!

CHAPTER TWELVE

Pat

Green Shoots and Shadows

2–24 October 2017

This second month revolves around school, home, CAMHS, baking scones, frantic tidying, therapy cooking (slow roast tomatoes anyone?) and spikes of sheer terror whenever the phone rings. Back in August, a new fireplace for roasting chestnuts seemed like a great idea. It is now a huge irritant, with hammer blows thundering through the walls while Jan and I have an adult conversation about the knock-on effect of our new life. It's surprisingly easy to agree that I cannot go back to work yet. We dare not broach how long *yet* is.

Although we are still reeling from the aftershocks of last month, more change is coming. We prepare a daunting list of questions about the handover from the Crisis Team to Community in CAMHS. Safety planning seems to rely on Dom (the boy who has debilitating social anxiety) telling someone if he feels suicidal. Armed with our two sides of A4 we are thwarted because Dom is in the meeting. 'Who do we contact if we are worried?' I ask.

'Us or go to A&E outside office hours.' That's it.

I meet Dom's new counsellor at their first session. He plunges right in and asks what my worries are. Christ, I can barely speak past the flood of fear. Acutely aware of Dom folded in by my side, I resist sobbing that I'm terrified he wants to kill himself. Composing myself, I tell the counsellor I'm worried that he hasn't got much support in place when all the underlying causes are still there. That Dom is up and down.

Pushing aside how selfish we feel, Jan and I steal four whole hours at a spa to celebrate our silver wedding anniversary alone. We know we must talk about absolutely nothing of consequence. Miraculously, by lunchtime, burying our heads in the sand has worked enough for us to share memories of our wedding day and, as we clink glasses to better times ahead, I manage a genuine smile and my heart lifts in response.

It sinks again when Dom chooses today to move back to his own attic room. After an exhausting argument with my own thoughts, I persuade myself that it is a sign of independence and put my effort into imagining that it all works out tickety boo from now on. When I force myself to go up there it is surprisingly light and calm.

Night thoughts

Has Dom killed himself and I have not heard? (I listened at the door to hear him breathing. I did not dare to go in and check so only succeeded in making the dog growl.)
Does Jan love me?
How will we get through if life is this hard?
How will we get the big desk out of the office?
What do I say to work?
Should I speak to my trusted fellow headteachers: Richard, Sue, Neil, or colleagues?
Will this ever end and will Dom get back to a normal life?
Is this a hot flush coming?
What do I say to the wider circle of friends and family?

Do I risk the truth?

Do I create a web of protective lies?

How the hell would I keep that up?

What are we going to do for money?

How do I get through to the people in CAMHS about the dark demons Dom is still fighting?

Will this churning sick worry ever end?

Is Greg really okay?

Is Dom any better?

And on and on and on and on and on and on and on and on.

The dawn has come; Jan has brought me hot tea and I can hear Dom singing in the shower.

School and CAMHS are the centre of gravity in each day and I have a ten-minute radius for expeditions out of the house, phone on full alert. My heart leaps at the ring tone on my phone (we've had a couple of calmer days). He's just left school. Mouth dry, mind frozen, I abandon a dog walk and race home to greet him. 'Hard,' is the reply to my enquiry about how the day has gone and he takes himself off for a bath.

Another day, I drive round town going nowhere to avoid bumping into people and eventually end up in the Marks & Spencer cafe seeking anonymous company but not conversation. I notice a missed call from the lovely student support manager at Dom's school. A rush of adrenaline spikes through me as I call back. No answer. The coffee tastes like poison as I sit watching the phone. After twenty minutes – a lifetime that is etched in my heart scars – she calls to say they've been chatting and he is struggling but has decided to stay. He seems bright enough by the end of the day while I am flattened with the never-ending anxiety of what ifs.

I brush off Jan's concern about how I am, unable to cope with the idea of another wheel falling off the wagon. We stagger on in this bleak alien landscape and irritating work responsibilities intrude again. After a tricky meeting with my employers, I realise I cannot win. People will feel let down whichever way I choose and deep down I could not live with myself if I prioritised work over home. For the first time in my life I cannot say yes to responsibility for anything else.

We make it to the weekend. Hurrah! We're going on a trip to Manchester for Dom to meet up with Immie in her new university digs. They hug tight in greeting and I watch as Dom morphs into his teenage cool self, although he throws me a look seeking reassurance, still not sure of himself. After checking the arrangements and charge on everyone's phone battery for a final time, Jan and I leave them to it, practically skipping with relief as we head off to the bright lights of the city centre for a precious few hours. We start our evening in The Alchemist and try out cocktails, stiffly acting the part of happy-go-lucky revellers and hoping the potion will lift our spirits. This buzzing crowd is a jolt after the last intense weeks. We have forgotten how to play and are strangers in this world where what you are wearing and who you are with seem to matter.

We move on and are more at ease over a quiet Chinese menu for two. We manage to reconnect, sharing concerns and feelings, despite both phones being face up on the table. The ping on Jan's phone jolts us back to the crappy reality of the situation. I know it is bad because he pales as he reads. 'What is it?' I press, already gathering my coat, bag and phone and half out of the chair. A thousand terrible visions race past me as we dash to find Dom and Immie at the teppanyaki restaurant around the corner.

By the time we arrive he has disappeared in a full-blown panic attack. The three of us scour the area, frantically texting Dom and eventually he replies that he is sitting on a bench in the nearby square on the edge of Chinatown. To my relief, Immie takes over, hugging Dom and chattering away until he is reassured. I sit numbly on the bench as the lights of Chinatown mock me with their promise of good times and Jan settles the bills in the restaurants. How can we even be thinking about future plans? I wish, again, that love was enough to solve it all.

After breakfast at the hotel and an emotional goodbye between Dom and Immie, we travel home in silence. At the kitchen table Jan and I dare, for a moment, to indulge in all the lovely normality of planning for a future after a meeting with school to discuss subjects, options and UCAS forms. But I can feel my hope ebb away as Dom and I walk and talk it over later, the red kites wheeling overhead throwing shadows on the ground. He says quietly that he does not know if he can handle the idea of university. 'Would you fancy a gap year like that?' I ask Dom, as we discuss the exciting plans of Chloe, one of his closest friends.

We walk on in silence until he replies: 'Not at this point in my life.'

Sadness overwhelms me and I struggle to find the right words, finally tucking his arm under my elbow. 'Try to be hopeful, my lovely; things will improve with the support you are getting.'

Monday 23 October

Pat to Kerry
Hi Fish, Tough weekend swinging between rock bottom and supernatural calm – I've detected a little brighter energy in Dom. Small smiles when a new scone recipe results in burnt bricks of dough. Deciding to stay off work has thrown me into a cleaning frenzy to fend off the resulting insecurity about my shrinking horizons. Yesterday I learned that the Chinese symbol for crisis is made up of two parts,

one signifying danger and the other hope. Which seems very fitting, though Dom did actually laugh this evening. Hurrah! Still, reality is really starting to sink in now and we've no idea where we are heading.

Kerry to Pat

Patti, I hear you. I get that feeling so much, that this is not a 'passing phase' but my bloody life. I've shouted at Cam today for his general belligerent attitude when we're trying to make things better. Now feel horrible as well as aggrieved that I'm doing everything possible to help but he can't even be bothered to remove his headphones to see if I have anything useful to say.

Tuesday 24 October

Pat to Kerry

Hi Fish, Hope I'm not waking you. Sitting in the waiting room again while Dom has his weekly appointment. Half term brings its own form of torture. He went for a walk on his own yesterday (having been very low all day). I have a very tidy filing cabinet as I was so agitated, I could barely resist stalking him down the street. Anyway, he came back so we soldier on. Hope things are okay with Cam and that the after-effects of last week aren't too bad. Hope you and Steve are okay too. It's just all so gruelling… Hope you've managed to find a bit of relax time – wish we were neighbours. xxxx

Kerry to Pat

Oh Patti I feel for you so much. Where to go with all this shit? It's so so so stressful. Who knew there was so much love inside us desperately trying to channel into our precious boys but hitting a breakwater of resistance every day? There will be life beyond this. Keep the faith. As people keep telling me, it will make us stronger people! My answer to that old chestnut is that if I wasn't already strong I wouldn't be able to get through it in the first place. Sending so much love your way. Xxx

Tuesday 24 October, 16.16
Hi Fish, Came across this today. Sums up mother love for me at the moment. Wanted to share. Hope it doesn't have an adverse effect as that is not what is intended. Lots of love to you all. Xxx

THE MORE LOVING ONE
Looking up at the stars, I know quite well
That, for all they care, I can go to hell,
But on earth indifference is the least
We have to dread from man or beast.

How should we like it were stars to burn
With a passion for us we could not return?
If equal affection cannot be,
Let the more loving one be me.

Admirer as I think I am
Of stars that do not give a damn,
I cannot, now I see them, say
I missed one terribly all day.

Were all stars to disappear or die,
I should learn to look at an empty sky
And feel its total dark sublime,
Though this might take me a little time.

WH Auden

Tuesday 24 October, 17.13

Christ, Patti, it so does sum up mother love but also a message of survival come what may. We'll get through this, my lovely. We will. Somehow. How did Dom get on? Are you coping? I feel really frayed at the edges now. Getting fed up with this being my normal life rather than my 'blip' life.

Had a very stressful day today as Cam needs a heart scan before the next chemo can go ahead (9/11) but they could only fit him in on 13/11. I threw myself on the secretary's mercy… 'Please, he's only seventeen, can you put me at the top of the waiting list?' God love her, she phoned me back this afternoon with an appointment for tomorrow. I thought I'd pass out with gratitude. We've also got a CT scan on Friday 3/11 which will tell us if the tumour is shrinking. Effectively, if the treatment is working. All hatches battened down until then. I've got a stinking cold, feel really, really rotten and don't even have the luxury of being ill – so stressed about giving it to Cam I'm bleaching the world around us. We'll all probably die of chemical inhalation instead…

Thanks for the poem. I like a bit of poetry.

Sending love. Hang on in there. And yep. So wish we were neighbours.

Xxx

Tuesday 24 October, 18.50

Oh bloody hell Fish, so much going on for you guys too and I really really am with you on the 'Thanks but no thanks to new normal – quite happy I've proved my resilience now thank you. Move on!'

Well done for swinging the heart scan. Sometimes I think the Fisher/Sowa stuff is just about using every available skill to try to get our way (when we know what we actually need or want from the system!). As for the scan on the 3rd… we will all be right by your side on that day/really wish we'd been able to come down but can't leave Dom… heading off to Cornwall tomorrow to see Greg. Have to say I am looking forward to looking at four different walls. xxx

CHAPTER THIRTEEN

Pat

A Change of Scene

25–28 October 2017

Dom is twitching and flushed, his eyes flicking from place to place without ever catching mine. Placing my hand gently on his knee to steady him, I ask what is wrong under my breath so as not to draw any more attention to us than necessary as the queue of people boarding the plane to Newquay look on. 'I hate this seat. Why do we always sit here?'

We always aim to sit in the front row (more leg room, less claustrophobia). 'What don't you like about it?' I probe.

'I hate the crew sitting opposite us. They look at me and you always talk to them.'

A profound sadness washes over me as I catch sight of the world through Dom's hyper-sensitive eyes. I am struck hard by his palpable knot of anxiety, how feeling constantly watched and judged must be so miserable and crippling for him. I tell him how sorry I am and that I wish he had been able to tell us sooner so that we could have picked different seats – not only on this trip but all of our flights. 'It's not your fault, Mum,' he replies and I think he means it. But it does not stop me sinking into a swamp of helpless guilt.

Later we sit basking at the beach bar, defending our lunch from the seagulls. I am absolutely determined that we are going to make the most of these precious few days which have been keeping me going over the last weeks. Greg and Dom are behaving like awkward strangers and I am the chirpy go-between. This parenting lark is much harder than I ever imagined. I survey the scene from the outside; it's not exactly a snapshot from *The Waltons*. I heave on the role of Family Red Coat and coax the boys out for a walk around the coast when, really, I would like to go to bed, pull the duvet over my head and whimper.

We stand for ages admiring the mighty waves pummelling the rocks and I breathe in the ozone. The Atlantic always makes my heart fill with joy. I'm surrounded by echoes from my childhood: big family holidays spent in North Devon, brother and sisters, cousins, aunts and uncles, buckets and spades, sandwich-spread rolls, windbreaks and bodyboarding. And fresher memories of my dad teaching our boys to fly a kite on the same beach. Innocent days that feel disconnected from our present reality. How can both be true?

Back at the hotel, we unpack in easy silence. The seaside appears to be working its magic on Dom too. My antenna has been constantly tuned to trying to read him so it is a luxury to know he is safely in sight for now.

But as the hours go by, my mood seems to be as changeable as the weather and too much time on my hands infects my mind with useless negativity that I do not have the energy left to fight. I'm unable to relax whenever Dom is out of my sight, exploring the coast and the town. I calm myself by remembering that CAMHS have set him the task of going out. I miss my friends who keep me grounded, squeeze out laughter from the depths of despair. Even a massage makes me tense and I race out, rejecting the offer of a relaxation room, to hunt for him. I search the hotel and grounds trying to keep breathing but when his head finally pops up from a sheltered nook I fold in half and the fear washes over me. I clench my hands in my pockets to resist the urge to limpet-cling to his arm.

It is a relief when Jan arrives for the weekend and we galvanise ourselves into organising activities interspersed with reading and constitutionals around the coast. We have mixed success, with everyone treading carefully around each other to avoid confrontations. A trip to St Ives in glorious October sunshine is aborted after Greg's ill-fated camper van breaks down. On the upside, we all rally around embellishing the *destined to fail day-trip saga* and Dom persuades Jan to take him to buy a second breakfast (a scone and cream – what else?).

In between these moments of laughter and normality there are darker shadows. As the three of them stride ahead on the springy grass, my tears well up at what we have come to. We are barely recognisable when I think back to the easy laughter and companionship of the summer. That was only fifty days ago and yet now we seem like a shattered ruin of a family and I am struggling to see how the future might unfurl. The mountain to climb between here and A-levels, let alone independence, seems too much of a challenge and we do not have the right equipment to hand.

> Pat to Kerry
> *Sea air is bracing but I am knackered. Can't tell if it is doing Dom any good and I'm terrified that he is telling us what he thinks we want to hear to keep us off his back.*

> Kerry to Pat
> *Must be impossible – mind reading not one of the parenting courses I've been on. Sending huge love. xx*

Saturday 28 October

The day before we are due to fly home, Greg and I tackle his grubby room, music on full blast and laughing as we sing and dance our way through the cleaning. I hate to interrupt this precious time together but I need to broach how he is and give him a chance to talk about what's going on with Dom.

'How are you feeling about everything?' is my opener. He talks about college and domestics, leaving the opportunity for deeper stuff untouched. Despite the brush-off, I persist in communicating that I'm here for him, that it's okay not to be okay, like a public service announcement until I annoy him.

'I'm alright, Mum. I have really good friends here and I will tell you if I need any help. You don't have to keep repeating yourself.'

I apologise, we hug and get back to our shared dancing and cleaning routine but I can tell the mood is broken.

Later on, while Dom's out for a walk. Jan and I sit out on the terrace making the most of the last rays of sunshine before we head home tomorrow. I push away the ceaseless worries of Dom being out of sight, returning to school and what happens next. As we are talking, an overwhelming sense of dread about Dom engulfs me and I leap out of the chair, run to his room, flinging open the door. I scan around: rucksack, books, ear phones, gym weights. Everything is in order. I gather myself in and head back to Jan. He asks if everything is alright and I nod, unable to articulate the terrifying vision of Dom that I have had. I talk firmly to myself: I am over-wrought, over-tired, overwhelmed. My imagination is running away with me. I text Dom: *Have you seen the sunset?*

Yes, I'm watching it now.

CHAPTER FOURTEEN

Pat

In the Still Morning at the Gates of Hell

29 October 2017

8.59

Mug of tea in hand, I tap on the door to wake Dom up in time for the flight home. As I open the door a strong breeze flows past me. The window is open and the curtains are wafting gently into the room, throwing shadows across the wall. Apart from the lazy flap of the curtains, all is silent.

'Dom?' No answer. The bathroom door is also open and I cannot see or hear him. Panic snakes upwards. Something is wrong. And then it gut-punches me. An abyss of dread opens before me. I call again and again, louder and more painful each time. The bed is crumpled. His phone is on the bedside table. His Rizlas too. I reel back towards Jan. I think I know but I grasp at rational alternatives. 'Have you seen Dom this morning?' My voice is high and thin; bile clags my throat. 'He's not here. He's gone.' Jan rushes through calling his name but there is only silence. We cling together as all the scaffolding of life collapses around us; 'We've lost him.'

The world is pinprick small and I cling onto the last threads of hope, although in my entrails I know. I know.

We divide to conquer: Jan heads out to hunt around the cottage as I race to the hotel reception. I am taken to a side room but my hands are shaking so much I cannot press the buttons on the phone so I pass it to the duty manager, Tom, to ring the police and he fills them in. He is suddenly my rescuer. The link to all our dreams of the future. The last shreds of possibility that there can be a happy ending. Maybe Dom is out walking? Stuck on the beach? I nod at the kind suggestions from a stranger but the mother in me knows.

Once the conversation with the police is over, Tom escorts me back to the privacy of our cottage and sits me down. It all happens very quickly but I am stuck in a parallel world of unimaginable pain. A time warp where every breath is an hour, every second stretched out to breaking point. A place where the route ahead has crumbled to dust. No Through Road.

The police arrive, competent, matter of fact, calm. I register kind eyes. I repeat all the details about Dom's struggles over the last few weeks as Jan arrives back, shaking his head and wild-eyed with fear. We sit on the sofa, shoulders pressed together, holding hands until they hurt as the detective in charge explains that the RNLI (Royal National Lifeboat Institution) and coastguard will be joining the search. I tell them that I fear the worst. They seek to reassure me that the most common outcome is that someone is found but it does not fully register. I cannot let go of hope but I cannot live by it either. I am balanced precariously on wanting the hope to win and this deep dread that I cannot shift.

The world moves into action around us. I am asked to describe his clothes and I go to his room to see if I can work out what he is wearing by checking what is still there. He's in black jeans, black coat, grey sweatshirt and his new walking boots. Doggie, his cuddly toy, has gone too. My heart thuds downwards as another guy rope to hope is abruptly severed.

The room is full of people and yet their voices are muffled; nothing can penetrate the solid wall of pain. My brain is failing to grasp the questions that are being asked, as if I have become deaf and mute. Sitting at the table wrapped in a blue woollen shawl, I find my limbs are frozen. And I wait. Every knock on the door quickly becomes a thing to dread. A possible death knell that makes every cell in my body lurch. I cannot allow myself to imagine a happy ending. The disappointment will be too much. It does not fit with the feelings that I cannot articulate.

While Jan goes with the police to fetch Greg to join us, I am unable to move. I sit for a lifetime… hours. I flinch as the door knocker is violently rapped and the silhouette of a policeman fills the doorway. He is carrying a black bundle. He comes towards me and I wrap my arms around my body tightly, fending off the moment. He asks if I recognise it. I nod; 'It's Dom's,' then I reach out and hold his coat close.

The police officer stands in the corner of the room, a watchful sentry, and I sit immobile, hugging Dom's coat, pressing my nose into the smell of him while the persistent throb of helicopters, motorboats and jet-skis fills the air of this otherwise silent space.

After another stretch of this immeasurable day, the policeman interrupts my paralysis to ask quietly if I could bring Dom's phone to him. As I hand it over I realise that the screen is not locked. I must have had some hope left until then because now I feel it seep away. His phone is always locked.

He intently scrolls through everything, stopping occasionally to walk away and speak to someone through the radio that has been crackling and spitting out words in the background. 'Can we speak to Dom's school, please?' I am thrown into a flurry of activity by making the phone call, which at least gives me something to do. Speaking to the head of sixth form is like visiting a former life – a place I cannot find the road back to. I should have left a trail of breadcrumbs.

I retreat from the conversation while the policeman digs around in Dom's phone, looking for clues, questioning Dom's friends and a teacher on the other end. He finally puts it aside and explains to me that they are pursuing other enquiries and need to check out the possibility of abduction. Do we know if Dom had arranged to meet anyone? 'We knew nothing about a Grindr account until I just overheard you, let alone a date,' I comment grimly.

Every muscle is screaming for action, filled with fight, flight and freeze chemicals that have nowhere to go. Jan, Greg and I are by turns prowling, sitting, scrolling through messages. Greg sets up a Facebook search and hands all the leads to the police. Hundreds of locals are looking for Dom. Caged in the cottage and its courtyard, I want to be out there hunting but the police ask us to stay where we are in case Dom turns up. They even ask me to send a friend home in case he turns up there. This is the boy who had forgotten we were catching a plane to Newquay this week. I'm not sure he could have found his way to the station, let alone back to our house.

Messages from helpless friends and family fill our phones and provide a welcome distraction even if they seem to come from a distant planet. *We are in hell*, I reply to the many *How are you?* messages.

The RNLI come and update us, a whirl of names and information. We are grateful; our future is in their hands – we scrape up the manners to say so. They are risking their own lives to save all of ours. But I cannot take up the offer to go and meet the crew because that would mean that all of this is real. If I just sit here, very still, it might be survivable.

CHAPTER FIFTEEN

Kerry

Happy Eighteenth Birthday

29 October 2017

The day before Cam's birthday is a bittersweet affair for so many reasons. The morning starts with heart wrench as we wave off some dear friends, Vanessa and Chris, who'd travelled all the way from North Wales to Surrey the day before to have one evening out with us. It's particularly poignant: we met them at Cam's National Childbirth Trust group all those years ago, and their daughter, Anna, was born a couple of weeks before Cam. We've holidayed together frequently and despite our busy lives and geographical distance, there's the sense that we really know and love each other's children. If anyone feels our pain, it's them. They're both health professionals and thankfully at ease with the cancer-dominated conversation, striking just the right note between sympathetic and curious that I feel I can be honest about how shit it's been. Despite the obvious difference between Anna's good health and Cam's pallor, we forgot about the cancer for a few short hours, their whole family lifting us as we reminisced about the kids as babies, life steadying for a moment, reminding us of who we once were.

Hugs and heartfelt hand squeezes over, we head off to London for afternoon tea with my extended family. I cannot get over the paradox of us all putting on our glad rags again as though this were just an ordinary day when next week, in five days' time, Cam will have the big scan that will tell us whether the treatment is working. I can't believe this might be the last birthday that he's here. It just seems so wrong. Steve and I get ready to perform, to chat and laugh and raise champagne. I'm nervous, afraid that seeing my mother and brother might snap the tiny toothpick holding back the floodgates. It's the first time Mum has seen Cam without hair – I've sent her photos to prepare her for how he looks now compared with the floppy-haired rugby player she last saw – and asked her to try and be brave in case it sets us all off.

I made the mistake of telling the restaurant that it was Cam's eighteenth and then had to phone back to say that under NO circumstances were they to sing to him – Cam hates being stared at because of his bald head. The idea of the whole of the restaurant putting down their cucumber sandwiches and slopping their Darjeeling, 'Happ-y birth-day to youuuu' dying on their lips as they realise, yes, that poor teenage boy has cancer, not a trendy haircut, would just about finish me off. Even without hair, in a suit and tie, he looks so handsome. The thick Fisher eyebrows are hanging on in there – for once, he's grateful for inheriting the hairy gene, though he's pretty grumpy that his chest and leg hair is hanging on with such alacrity.

We sit in the taxi heading towards Regent Street when Jan, Pat's husband, rings Steve. I can't hear Jan's side of the conversation, just the cadence of desperation that words have when disaster strikes. I know by Steve's face that there's bad news. The call is short.

Steve fills me in. 'Dom's missing. There's a coastguard search for him. I could hear the helicopters flying overhead.'

We sit in silence for the rest of the journey. I can't get away from the image of Patti sitting with her face pressed against the window, waiting for news. A text seems almost disrespectful. I decide something is better than nothing.

Kerry to Pat
Patti, I'm here for you and inadequately sending love. I cannot imagine what you are going through.

The answer is hell comes straight back.

At the hotel, I try to concentrate on the here and now. The words, the conversation, flow around me, while I wonder. Is Dom back? Have they found him? In between, we toast Cam; no one cries. We talk about how lovely the scones are, how the champagne will go straight to Cam's head as he hasn't had a drink in three months and despite the questions clanging into my mind like protesters holding up billboards – Will Cam die? Will Dom be okay? – the afternoon has a veneer of normality. I wonder what will be left of any of us when this is all over, whichever way it goes.

CHAPTER SIXTEEN

Pat

The Sky Goes Dark

29 October 2017

Late in the day my big sister Janet and my brother Michael arrive. We hug and sob, hearts broken. Janet tries to offer reassurance that he will turn up but hard as I try (does it make me a bad mother if I give up hope?) I cannot see this being true. Otherwise they would not be here, would they?

The hotel duty manager has spent the day standing in the corner of the room, a steady discreet presence emanating calm kindness and who has somehow anchored us all by invisibly organising tea, sandwiches, wine, bedrooms for the family. The police have been with us too and at first I thought they were looking after us but it crosses my mind that maybe we are being guarded.

Pat to Kerry
We are beyond despair and the search is still on but will stop at dark. Jan and I both fear the very worst and think we have lost him. Will send news.

Kerry to Pat
I don't know what to say, Pat. Our hearts are with you. xxx

The sky falls dark and silent as the helicopters and search parties head home. We grimly talk ourselves to a standstill. Greg heads back to his own bed and late into the night Janet and Mike steer us towards ours to sleep the impossible sleep. Jan is fitfully resting beside me and Dom's coat is curled up between us like a toddler. I lie awake in the stillness and think of my boy. I try to will him alive with my mother love. But as my tired and bruised heart searches for hope, a coldness creeps over me. It dawns on me that there might be worse things than finding his body. Because the alternative of never knowing might just be worse.

CHAPTER SEVENTEEN

Kerry

This Isn't How I Planned It

30 October 2017

Having cancer has not dimmed Cam's enthusiasm for birthdays. He still bounces out of bed to open his cards and presents with the joy of a ten-year-old. He's oddly touched by the photo albums I've made for him and doesn't seem to have any of the heartache I feel at looking back over happier, healthier times. We all join in singing 'Happy Birthday' but my mind keeps drifting to Cornwall, wondering what the news is, whether this morning will bring relief or disaster. Although I've railed against the injustice that Cam is celebrating his birthday with a blood test at the Marsden, Pat and Jan's situation underlines yet again that there's always someone worse off. I check my phone for news but the screen remains resolutely blank.

At the hospital, I give Cam a couple of presents I've brought with me as a distraction while we wait for his arms to heat up under the electric warmer so his veins are more easily accessible. After he's opened his cufflinks, the nurse starts the whole rigmarole of trying to find a way in. The poor boy has inherited my inaccessible veins and he lives in fear of having to have another PICC line put in. We've already been told that very few people make it to the end of treatment without one. Cam has never got over his fear of needles, despite all the blood tests and cannulas. He looks away, his eyes screwed up against the nurse tapping to try and find somewhere to suck out the blood, which will tell us if his neutrophils are good enough for chemo next week.

But today, we're in luck. The process is swift and Cam is thrilled with the twenty-pound note that comes in a card from all of the nurses. In the whole bad luck of Cam getting cancer in the first place, we had the good luck to live twenty minutes from the Marsden, in a country where healthcare is free at the point of access. The nurses, all of them, are cheery and helpful. God knows how they manage that day in, day out.

I can't bear it any longer. Now Cam's blood test is over, I have to know what is happening down in Cornwall. I text Pat from the tiny pocket of hospital where there is a signal, hoping I'm not intruding.

> Kerry to Pat
> *Thinking about you all the time and hoping today brings good news. This feels very inadequate in the face of what you are going through.*

She responds, *No news. We are trying to prepare ourselves. Happy birthday to Cameron. Hope you are all drinking champagne.*

I've never felt less like it.

CHAPTER EIGHTEEN

Pat

We Are In Hell

30 October 2017

I must have dozed off because I am woken up by the already familiar soundtrack of the search: the grumble of the helicopters and whine of jet-skis interrupted by the squawk of the gulls on the roof. Feeling sick with the knowledge of what today might bring, I force myself out of bed to face it, taking Dom's coat with me as a talisman.

The hell that we have been living in continues with a hideous rhythm all of its own. The police, the updates, the stuttering radios. I sit frozen on the sofa, my poncho pulled over my head. Maybe if they cannot see me, I cannot be found and if they cannot find me, they cannot tell me.

Greg's Facebook search has thrown up a possible lead and there is a flurry of hope as the search teams follow it up. I cannot bear to dash the look in his eyes but I know. I just know.

I send some messages to the world I no longer feel part of while there is constant activity around us: police officers come and go and the hotel staff bring breakfast, which is left untouched on the table. The intensity of the crackled conversations on the radio increases and more police arrive, along with a man in yellow wellies who must be from the RNLI. I retreat back under my comfort blanket on the sofa.

Janet, Mike, Jan, Greg and I are cooped up in the cottage with the police and the hotel duty manager. A policeman asks us to turn off our phones, put down the iPad. I register an intensity and level of seriousness in his tone that tells me we are nearing the point of no return. All hope gone.

From the stasis of the last twenty-six hours everything bursts into frenzied activity as if someone has lit an invisible touchpaper. The detective in charge of the search bursts into the cottage and asks us to sit down. Greg is between Jan and me and we take each other's hands. Three in a row.

He is panting heavily and apologises, 'I had to run to beat the social media.'

How am I still breathing? This cannot be.

He explains that they have found a body in the sea. That it will need to be identified but that it is a young male. The three of us cling together, heads bent against this news as my world compresses to a pinprick of light and then explodes into a million shards of pain.

CHAPTER NINETEEN

Kerry

In the Lap of the Gods

30 October–3 November 2017

The news comes in at lunchtime. They've found Dom's body.

Kerry to Pat
*I could be with you by tomorrow afternoon if any use? As a
friend, I am at a complete loss to know what to do for you so tell
me what you need when you are ready to think about it. I will
do anything, anything at all to help. My heart goes out to you.*

Pat to Kerry
*Thank you so much. We are absolutely reeling. Staying here
for a few days with Greg, and my brother and sister are
here, so much as I'd love to see you, let's save it for when
the initial numbness and chaos have worn off.*

Wednesday 1 November

Kerry to Pat
*Just giving you some space without hundreds of 'thinking of
you' texts because you might feel like shouting at the world
to fuck right off, but we ARE thinking of you.*

Pat to Kerry
I'd love to talk and will call when I am capable of it.

Kerry to Pat
You call any time. And that's really an ANY time. I don't sleep well so the chances are you won't be waking me up. Don't lie there feeling like the loneliest person in the world. Love you both.

On the third of November, Cam and I drive separately to the Marsden for the scan halfway through his treatment to see whether it's working. Steve finds it weird that we go in two cars but I understand. Cam just wants to deal with his own emotions without having to think about mine. It feels like a huge roll of the dice while we sit there waiting his turn. Apart from the cough that stopped very early on as the steroids shrunk the tumour, we have no idea whether Cam has responded or not. As he is called in, I'm aware that it's yet another experience for him to push down into that deep dark place.

In the waiting room, another patient, a man in his sixties, says, 'Your boy's young to have cancer.' His tone is too kind and I start to mumble something about random bad luck but my throat gets clogged with sadness and the emotions I've been hiding from Cam burst out. The man's face takes on the horror of having upset me, the panic of 'Where's my wife when I need her?' etched on his features.

I apologise and say, 'Give me a minute,' whip out my eye whitening drops and plaster a smile back on as though that huge swell of grief that my boy is in there, right now, with someone knowing whether or not the odds are tilting in our favour was just a little frippery, like getting distraught over your football team losing.

We find our safe ground in talking about where Cam is applying for university. I blather on about distance from home, how we haven't yet visited any. I don't say that none of us can be bothered to look at universities because we've no idea whether he'll still be alive to go. Instead I tell him that Cam is going to Ayia Napa after his A-levels with seventy of the people from his year. I can't imagine my bald boy with his round steroidy face, this lad for whom pâté, live yoghurt and salami pose a threat, ever being well enough to drink shots and party into the small hours in eight months' time – however much I'd like to.

Cam arrives back and while we wait for the regulation half an hour to check he doesn't have a reaction to the chemicals they pump into him for the scan, we discover the man has been cancer-free for six years but continues to have a check-up every year. I wonder if he still thinks about having had cancer every day, or whether it just bobs into his consciousness now and again when something reminds him. I never get to ask as Cam suddenly jumps to his feet, grabs his stuff and says, 'I'm going back to school.' He marches off without waiting for me. There's no recognition that this is hard for me too but I can't blame him for not having the headspace to consider anyone else. As often happens at the end of the conversation with any patient at the Marsden, the man and I wish each other good luck. Not good luck as a social nicety but *good luck* with real heartfelt sentiment behind it, united by our understanding of how precarious life is.

I head out to the car and prepare for the longest six days of my life until we're back here again for the results.

At home, I find a long text from Pat, warning me not to read the next bit 'if you need not to cry'. I sit and absorb her account of the lovely hotel staff, the kindness of the RNLI man who found Dom. I'm struck that even in the midst of tragedy there is still goodness to be found in the world. She asks about Cam and I text back a simple, *No idea until next week. Wish you were here to hug. Let us know when we can help.* Only a really special person could be generous enough to ask about Cam when Dom is lost to her forever.

CHAPTER TWENTY

Pat

The Kindness of Strangers and Friends

30 October–4 November 2017

Monday 30 October

Kerry to Pat
*Glad you have company. We are here when you are ready
for us, with whatever you need. X*

Pat to Kerry
*Thanks Fish. We really have no map for this. Stomach
churned. Brain shot. Lots of love to you all.*

Kerry to Pat
*No one has a map for this and I so wish you didn't need
one either. We're here. XX*

The police give us time alone after breaking the news but come
back in the early evening to explain the procedures. Dominic is
a child in the eyes of the law now. My eyes lock onto his, daring
him to look away. How can that be? So when he was alive and
under CAMHS he was an adult but now he's dead he's my child

again? I know I am ranting but I cannot stop. 'It's unforgivable. Perverse. If it were your child, you wouldn't stand for it.' The detective looks uncomfortable but stays silent.

He goes on to explain as gently as he can that the coroner will need someone to identify the body formally. This thrusts me back into the reality of Dom's death and I run from the room to escape the knowledge and the responsibility. There is no parenting handbook for this.

Jan and I discuss what to do, trying to make our shit-for-brains work through the shock. My Irish side, the part of me that wants to honour Dom by seeing him one last time, tells me to go to the mortuary. But I am terrified of a cold white room and an image that will burn into my soul. I'm not sure I have the required courage. The immovable fact that someone has to do this means we cannot defer the decision (and anyway, how long would be long enough?). My brother heroically offers to go instead but I cannot allow someone else to be there if I am not, to see him, touch him, kiss him when I do not. After a long silence, hopeless tears falling, we are rescued by the detective, who takes pity on us. He suggests that he talk to the coroner's assistant to see if they are willing to let him identify on our behalf using photographs. Thank God for this man's humanity.

My school emergency training kicked in at some point after the transition from waiting to knowing. The first people I call with the news are his friend Immie's parents so they can collect her from university and keep her safe. The second person is the head of sixth form. I want him to be able to prepare for what to say in school tomorrow. We agree that he will bring Dom's friends together, try to look after them. I discover that saying the words out loud is a knife blade in my heart. The feelings are stoppered in my throat but speaking threatens to release a flood that may sweep me away. So my brother handles the family round robin. I speak to some people but have no idea who or what words we exchange. Nothing seems to register.

In the evening, there is a steady flow of strangers who want to pass on their condolences. We are in a family hotel; the staff have a knack of being calm and compassionate, unfussy. Just kind. The visits make me acutely aware of how dishevelled we are. It has all gone to pot but I cannot find it in myself to be bothered. There is no space for anything beyond the anguish. The quiet rhythm of visitors who talk to us about Dom keeps the hysteria at bay. Just.

I'm catatonic on the sofa when my sister leads me to bed in the early hours of the morning. I ask her to leave the light on in the hallway. I cannot bear the darkness. It seems like a betrayal to rest so I fight sleep and when I finally succumb, my dreams are filled with terrible visions. My body convulses, heaving with dry sobs. I feel Dom's spirit leave me, a reverse birthing, dark matter pulling away from me. And I receive a crystal-clear message that I have to set him free. This feeling remains with me when I awake.

Tuesday 31 October (Samhain, Halloween, The Day of the Dead, the date of my father's death)

The day after Dom's body was found, the weather is beautiful. The sky is a cloudless vivid blue, the sea is calm and there is not a breath of wind. It is warm enough to sit outside in shirtsleeves. The glorious setting jars cruelly with our ragged emotions when Jan, Greg and I go for a walk together along the coast. Janet, my sister, has been steering us towards going out for walks when the claustrophobia of the rooms becomes unbearable. The space outdoors becomes overwhelming in its own turn so we rotate, flailing between the two for something that soothes us.

Dom was a nature boy and already I feel comfort out in the elements. A seal pops its head up in the bay and later a dolphin. They are talking to me, sending messages from eternity, setting all of this horror in the cycle of life and death. The waves never cease to play the same tune: all things will pass; there is a time for everything and nothing stays the same. The world sings to its own rhythm and we are a tiny part of the orchestra. Feeling my insignificance somehow helps.

As we walk Greg says, 'Dom did not do this to hurt us.' We open up, talking about our confusion, questions and pain, and it helps. We agree to try to live life to the full, just as Dom wanted to. We have to live his life through ours now.

There is no way on earth that this is what Dom wanted. We talk about how what has happened is not right. Dom was ill; he did not want to die, he just did not know how to live. The lack of proper help, the treatment that could have saved his life, just was not there. The view in hindsight is searingly bright and we can only spend so much time discussing the 'if onlys' before it hurts too much. Beyond it all, the instinctive belief that he loved us gives us a banner around which to gather and face the future.

Time is moving in parallel, unconnected to my experience. It is a meaningless concept as I attempt to find my footing without Dom. I spend the night on a task I cannot believe I am asked to do. On my laptop, I scroll through a slide show of our summer holiday a lifetime ago, trying to find the photos which show the marks that identify Dom: the mole on his back, the birthmark on the side of his neck, the scar from his first chicken pox spot. The one freckle on the end of his nose that he wanted to get rid of. I am sitting outside myself as I do this, forcing myself to focus on the job in hand. Eventually I send the file of photos to the coroner's assistant. It's better than a mortuary visit.

More practicalities of death begin to creep in. We have to arrange a funeral director to transport Dom's body home. We want a non-religious funeral (Dom was very clear on his views about this). The first two undertakers (people who take you under?) leave me cold but the third is a woman and she cries. I cry with her and know she is the one. I cannot bear the thought of Dom going home without me and am nowhere near ready to leave Greg here. We agree to aim for the next weekend, as long as the coroner will release his body. This date puts the rest of the week into a frame and my sister makes plans to go home on Thursday. The hotel staff suggest we move into a room in the main building and it's a good idea: a first step away from where hope of a happy ever after ended.

Life seems so fragile. It turns on a sixpence and, for us, will never be the same. *One day at a time, sweet Jesus.* These country and western lyrics swing through my mind. I cling on to them. In fact, I latch on to anything I can find to keep me anchored.

Jan and I talk over who could officiate at a funeral like this. We google humanists but they seem so detached from our reality. I can almost see Dom grimacing. The idea of a stranger being the one to shepherd us through such an intimate, vulnerable event is not very appealing. Jan wants Neil Renton, the head of sixth form. He has been kind, calm, compassionate and I immediately agree. We phone him together, nervous of a no but Neil interrupts before we have even finished asking to say he would be honoured. I am in awe of the people who seem to know how to help us. I'm not sure I would be anywhere near as good at it.

Wednesday 1 November (All Saints' Day)

The ballroom at the hotel is laid out with white tablecloths and set for a wedding. Staff members are gathered in sociable groups, though as we walk into the room the chatter drifts away to a respectful silence. Jan and I sit holding hands as the manager thanks us for coming. That night, for the first time, I talk about Dom. Who he was, his love of music, art and baking. We share photographs and the staff come to hug us, touch our hands, say how sorry they are for our loss. The ability of these people to be alongside us at this time is humbling. We feel blessed to be here.

Strangers (I think of them as angels) appear from nowhere and become friends in this new unwanted life. Some of our dearest long-term friends become our lifesavers, keeping us together and helping to create a link between our past and our future world. Others, perhaps with their own stuff going on, become distant or even disappear – I wonder if they think it is catching?

> Pat to Kerry
> *Don't read the next bit if you need not to cry.*
> *Jan, Greg and I are learning to grieve. We had a difficult but very moving evening when the RNLI crew came specially to meet us. They talked about how they found Dom and I was able to meet the men and women who found him. They have offered to be with us if we return for any part of our grieving.*

My brother and sister come to meet the lifeboat crew too. They have their own sadness to deal with though I can barely register anything beyond my own bewilderment. We are surrounded by folk of the sea who comfort me with their presence, the sense that they have seen tragedy and have strength to spare for us. One of them shares his own struggles with mental health as his crew mates listen in silence, never having realised before. I hold the hand of Peter, the man who brought Dom to the lifeboat, with both of mine. This last physical link to Dom is overwhelming. Eventually I manage to let go.

Thursday 2 November

My big sister and I sit on a bench overlooking the waves as they pound the shore. She gives me a tree of life bracelet that had been intended for Dom, the other for Greg. I put it on and we clutch each other and sob our goodbyes. When my nephew, who has come to drive her home, arrives, he wraps me in a bear hug, which gives me just enough strength to wave them off and then I retreat back to the bench.

Greg's landlord and landlady, Simon and Yvonne, have asked if they can meet with us before attending Simon's son's graduation. I actually cannot believe that someone would do this. That they would travel out of their way to meet two complete strangers and I am one hundred per cent sure that I would not have done the same. People we don't know are easier than friends and family. I do not have the capacity to carry the grief of others who knew and loved Dom. It's better to be with someone who brings a little distance along with their compassion. Simon talks of his own love of the sea. He tells us that when we touch the water we will be touching Dom (this helps me immediately, as I had flinched cleaning my teeth). Yvonne and he offer to look out for Greg and I leap on the suggestion greedily. I am dreading leaving him alone.

Jan and I are both physically exhausted so one of the hotel's many angels in disguise arranges a massage for each of us. I manage the half hour although my mind cannot stop circling Dom's last moments. My muscles are painful with the strain of holding myself together but I do feel a tiny bit better, a little more grounded afterwards.

Saturday 4 November

Yesterday, Dom's body was taken back to Yorkshire and now we must follow. I have to hope I find a bit of willpower to walk away from Greg and from this place that will be forever in my heart. The week ends with a surreal firework display; we are raw with grief and cling on to each other alongside my brother, as the rockets whizz and flare. Sending messages to the sky. My mum and dad and now Dom all died around Bonfire Night. My childish love of sparklers has been extinguished by loss and I am not sure it will ever rekindle in the same way.

This is a week out of time. Unhinged from any other reality. Learning to walk in a new world where we are strangers to ourselves: talking, crying, memories of Dom, navigating being a three, organising a funeral for my child, preparing to return home, booking flights, moving away from the scene and into the hotel, finding a GP, sleeping tablets, diazepam. And all of it under the physical weight of the most desperate sorrow. The empty space where Dom should be.

Dealing with disappointing/disappearing friendships

Everyone says you will be surprised by the impact on friendships when life takes a sharp and painful turn and that was our experience too. Some people will step up to the plate and others will run away and hide in the understairs cupboard. It seemed easier to accept the latter if we looked behind the behaviour. (Although sometimes we just decided we couldn't find the energy to be bothered and let the friendship drift.)

- Embarrassment can make people stay away. There's also the fear that they wouldn't know what to say, that they'd say the wrong thing, that we'd be too busy to respond to their message, that they'd be interrupting us when we had bigger things to worry about. As long as people accepted that we might not be able to reply immediately, we found it comforting to know that people were thinking about us. People were also frightened that they'd make a fool of themselves by crying when we were being strong or that we'd cry and they wouldn't know how to comfort us.
- It seemed particularly galling (and it hurt) that people who'd been friends for decades, who'd watched our children grow up, vanished as though suicide or cancer might be contagious. Other more peripheral acquaintances surpassed themselves with offers of help.
- Our conclusion is that a friend's ability to be there for you relates to how comfortable they are around emotion – effectively, their tolerance for other people's pain. Knowing this might or might not help you accept it.

- Some people didn't say anything because they didn't want to remind us. They couldn't 'remind' us because we'd never forgotten but ignoring the topic made us feel that they were indifferent. It emphasised the feeling that it was our job to find our happy faces so we didn't make other people uncomfortable.

Kerry
'I really appreciated anyone who was brave enough to say, "How's Cam?" even if they had no idea what the answer would be. It felt like a gesture of generosity – "I'm prepared to take a risk to let you know I care."'

- If you've always been the stronger person in the friendship/ the one who makes all the effort/the one who fixes things, it might be that the relationship doesn't work when the roles are reversed and you are the needy one.
- Some people are particularly good at stepping up during a crisis but fade away, sometimes dramatically, when it's over.
- Often support came from friends who'd known tragedy themselves and no longer feared it because they knew it was possible to survive.
- Some people thought that talking about how devastated they were at our news – how much they'd cried, how they couldn't sleep – demonstrated how much they cared, whereas to us, if it got too intense, it almost felt as though they were asking for our support and sympathy at a time when it was all we could do to hang together ourselves.
- Some friendships never recover – the distance created by the experience is too far to cross. On the upside, you might find that because of the magnitude of what you've been through, losing a friend doesn't matter as much as you thought it would.

- Accept that people who say unhelpful or unkind things don't mean to be malicious. You might not forget it, but with time, you might be able to accept it as thoughtless or clumsy, rather than deliberate.

Pat

'It took me over a year to notice that I hadn't heard from some friends. It's made me realise that the balance of friendships can be fragile and I have not had the capacity to be the one who drives the relationships in the aftermath of losing Dom.'

Kerry

'An acquaintance who'd bumped into Cam in town said, "Cameron told me you've been crying all the time." I had cried. A lot. But here's the thing, I hadn't cried anywhere near as much as I wanted to. I'd sat dry-eyed while litres of poison clicked into him. I'd held myself in and hugged him when he'd had to stay behind while all his friends went nightclubbing in London without him. I'd watched him cheer on his rugby team from the sidelines, so frustrated at not being on the field, without shedding a tear because I wanted to show him that we were strong, that we could get through this. And all the time my heart had been breaking. Her saying that made me feel as though I'd been weak, that I'd failed, at a time when it was essential that I didn't let him down. It's the first thing I think about whenever I see her, even now.'

CHAPTER TWENTY-ONE

Pat

Now We Are Three

5 November 2017

Surf relentlessly thunders onto the rocks fringing the coast below our hotel window. This is the soundtrack to my packing. I gather the contents of my suitcase back in and squish hard on the lid. Then I carefully place Dom's belongings into his kit bag so we can carry them home.

Sensing a meltdown gathering, I quickly knock back a diazepam, unable to keep myself stitched together without help: I don't like the comatose koala effect it has on me and never thought I would take drugs but I have to say goodbye to Greg and leave him here to fend for himself.

We take a last walk along the headland under a looming storm and talk through Greg's back-up plans: the GP, his friends, Simon and Yvonne. Or to be more accurate, I download a tsunami of advice into the wind while Greg tips me a nod occasionally, trying and failing to reassure me that he will be fine. I'm acutely aware of my unattractive needy parenting but that doesn't help me change tactics. I'd never forgive myself if I didn't say it all now.

*

The three of us have a farewell lunch together overlooking the near empty beach. We raise a toast to Dom and to each other with more than a hint of stoic hysteria. We take a family photograph for the first time without Dom and somehow each of us dredges up a smile to please the camera – instinctively, we need to send each other a message that we are going to be alright, that we have one another to draw courage from. I deliberately choose a shot with the sea behind us to anchor us in this place, this moment where life has to turn a page whether we like it or not.

Greg hugs each of us in turn then we all get in the car, which Tom, the duty manager who's been by our side all week, has offered to drive. We drop Greg at his student digs. In the end, the act of leaving is dictated by the fact that we are running a bit late and I'm strapped in the back of the car: a squeeze of the hand, traded 'I love you's, an entreaty to call us any time and he is gone, the gate banging shut behind him.

Jan and I sit in silence, shoulders pressed together, as we conjure up some strength to get through this unwanted homecoming.

The house has been empty for over a week and exists in a land that I cannot return to regardless of the geographical reality. The flight passes in a blur. My imagination sees darkness: gloomy cold rooms devoid of life.

Reasons to return:

1. Our friends are waiting.
2. Dom's body is there.
3. Where else would we go?

While we've been away our friends have been in constant touch, twining a thread of love and hope between us and home. It is this thread that now draws us back.

After baggage reclaim, Jan and I prepare ourselves behind the shaded glass screens that stand between us and reality. We've been buffered during our week away but now we are entering a new phase. It's the moment we face becoming enforced empty nesters, brutally thrust into learning to live in a house without children.

Much as we'd like to, we can't stay here forever so eventually, in silent agreement, we grip hands and step through, the doors sliding back as we are scooped up by dear friends who hold us together when we collapse in their arms.

I've tried to ready myself for stepping over the threshold of the house but have not been able to imagine physically doing it. I hadn't factored in the dog, who goes bananas with joy, leaping, rolling over and licking our faces in greeting. The house is filled with a warm glow: every candle lit, all the fairy lights found. The dining table is set and a welcoming committee made up of nearly all of our closest friends is draped in casual groups about the rooms. The lengths these people have gone to are incredible. In the unluckiest of situations, we are lucky that our friends are definitely not of the fairweather variety. The kitchen is filled with the aroma of hearty food – the fish pie so kindly made at Jan's request in the careful planning of our return. We can't handle surprises right now so everything has been shared and discussed beforehand.

Maybe because of this, against the odds, we can sit around a table laden with food, wine and love. We share our week, what we know of what's happened. We hear of their own sobbing, sadness and shock and it makes us feel a bit less alone in this darkest time. And with infinitesimal shifts we begin to reconnect to parts of who we were before – parts that might survive in this new harsh and very bumpy terrain. It's our friends who keep the conversation going when we falter and who hold our pain as we alternate between silence, tears, confusion and yes, even a little unforced laughter.

Further reasons to return:

1. Caragh the dog.
2. This is where we belong, where we are known: our family home.

CHAPTER TWENTY-TWO

Kerry

The Spin of the Roulette Wheel

9–10 November 2017

As we sit at the Marsden waiting for the results, Cam has retreated into himself, ignoring everyone and focusing on his phone. I don't know where to put my thoughts. I try not to look at the faces of the other parents in the room, trapped in their own misery, mired in a problem that they might not be able to fix, where love, money and force of desire count for nothing. The kids that really break my heart are the little ones, excited to play with the Wendy house with its inscription, 'A small thank you for the big thing you've done', too young to have any idea about what the bastard disease means for them and their families. My palms seem to have a water supply of their own. I keep wiping them on my trousers but they bubble up again like mountain springs. The consultants are in and out, calling in parents who are all hoping for a miracle. Our oncologist appears and disappears, acknowledges us. We're trying to read her. Does she look happy to see us? Guarded? What must it cost her to keep her face neutral, whatever the news, until we get into that room for Judgement Day.

Finally, it's our turn. She puts us out of our misery immediately. 'It's excellent news.'

The tumour has shrunk by sixty per cent, down from a fat 10 cm by 8 cm to something much smaller, which could even be scar tissue. Steve sits, his face impassive, though I know it's all going on inside. Cam and I have enough emotion for everyone in the room, bursting into tears then laughing hysterically. She reassures us further, quoting from the report 'an excellent response to treatment', which apparently is a phrase they use sparingly. I send a blanket text to everyone with the good news. Steve goes home and Cam and I go for his next chemo. The six hours ahead don't seem anywhere near as arduous now we know it's working. We're careful not to talk too loudly or look too happy as we walk over to the outpatient ward.

Not everyone has results like this.

As I sit watching the poison pump into Cam, hope seeps into the cracks where despair lay this morning. I wonder how Pat and Jan are coping with our news when their own is so painful. A text full of champagne corks arrives from Pat, followed by an email from Jan just before we leave for home:

Thursday 9 November, 19.19
Hi Steve and Fish
    Have got back from meetings all day and following up my brief text I just wanted to say it was absolutely fantastic to get the news on Cam today – it really lifted me, and I hope you celebrate properly tonight! Get that wine in! All our love to you, Jan xx

Friday 10 November, 08.35
Hi Jan and Pat
    I'm so touched by your generosity of spirit – the fact that you even have the emotional capacity to think about anyone else at the moment humbles me. We were so relieved to hear

that Cam is on the right path – still a long way to go but very glad he isn't sitting through all that chemo for no benefit.

Your JustGiving page is doing brilliantly – I've shared it on my FB page and donated this morning. It feels so wrong to say I hope you're all coping and other crappy platitudes. The English language suddenly seems so lacking in words to express the deep feelings in my heart, my desire to comfort, my admiration for your strength and, frankly, my profound sadness that you've lost such a lovely boy and all that entails for your family. I hope, even without finding the right words, that you will know that we are here for you, not just in this initial stage of your grief, but forever. So many people have said to us, 'You can call any time, even in the middle of the night' and I've literally looked at them and thought, I wouldn't call you at 11 a.m., let alone 3 a.m. Well, I hope we can be the friends that you would call at 3 a.m.

Sending huge love to all of you.

Kerry xxxx

Friday 10 November, 08.53
Fish
You're such fab, fab friends and just get it completely. I cried and then burst out laughing at your 'wouldn't call you at 11 a.m.' comment – you've always been able to do that.

It will be great to see you on the two days of Dom's funeral but I know the real time with you will be after that. Loads of love to you all, Jan xx

CHAPTER TWENTY-THREE

Pat

Crumbs of Comfort

Mid-November

Thursday 16 November, 9.05
Think helpful thoughts. Be kind to yourselves and set small
goals to get you through each day. With love to you all, Andy.

Our friend has sent an email on hearing the news and it ends with these lines. They strike a chord, cutting through the thick wall of pain for both me and Jan. It seems random what gets through to us as we are grappling with our emotions, throwing everything we have ever learned about ourselves, this human existence, at survival and sanity.

I print the words in a large, bold font, cut them out and stick them all over the house: on every mirror and in every room so that we have a focus, a reminder to keep going. It would be so easy, natural, expected even, for us to turn to the wall, for our souls to shrivel in the acid of loss and to retreat from the world never to be seen again.

Our friends have rallied round and organise a rota to stay with us, providing some ballast to our rocky boat. They cook, clean, shop, distract and comfort us. Cups of tea are placed in my hand no matter how often I leave them undrunk. And we allow routine (clean teeth, shower, dress) to steer us through the indistinguishable days.

For the first weeks, I cannot think beyond the next minute, let alone the hour or day. Every thought drains me of energy, and decision-making is impossible. I have never felt more vulnerable and am so grateful for the incredible people who shift their own lives around us to stay overnight (darkness is overwhelming when we are alone and the demons gain strength in our tiredness). Jan has to carry on with work (part of his sanity) but I cannot venture beyond my own edges. Gradually, the outside world imposes itself but I cannot think about my job and have to leave it to others to sort out. Nothing matters beyond surviving, finding a way to carry on through the pain which has engulfed every thought, every bone, nerve and organ in my body.

My borders have shrunk to the house and garden. Venturing downstairs is a mission almost impossible. The bird feeder that Dom and I built so recently connects me to him and I tend it religiously, obsessed with the idea that I must keep the starlings, great tits and robin alive. There's snow on the ground so I go out in wellies, Puffa jacket and pyjamas twice a day. Our feathered friends have never had it so good and as the news passes around ever more of them gather. I spend hours watching them through the window, tears quick to flow as I wish pointlessly for a return to the times Dom and I did the same thing together.

'Look at you. You're dressed!' I am standing in Waitrose. For the first time I have managed to go into the shop. I have tried before but each time a rising panic has trapped me in the car and I have returned home exhausted. Getting this far today is a major achievement. And, of course, I've bumped into someone who knows me. My bark of laughter catches both of us by surprise. My tongue is tied with the effort of not collapsing and I have no outer skin. I've been stripped bare of the usual phrases and facades that belong to another time, to another me. She lays a kind hand on my forearm. 'I don't know how you get out of bed in the mornings. Let me know if I can help in any way.' With a tight grimace, I scuttle off before she sees the tears fall.

Saturday 18 November, 07.36
Hi Fish, woke up feeling ridiculously angry with all the stupid stuff people say to me. Feel like sending them all a ranty round robin. Am sending it to you instead:

Dear friends and neighbours and anyone else who knows me,
    I know I sound hideously ungrateful when I should be glad you've been brave enough to talk to me at all given that apparently some folks think suicide is catching. To be fair, most people get it more or less right but there are some things NOT to say to me when my son has died by suicide.

- *'He is in a better place now.' Really? No words. Home was quite nice, thank you.*
- *'He was too good for this world.' No, he was not. He was a typical teenager, a pain for not telling me where he was going, and his bedroom was like a charity shop in a tornado. But he was my typical teenager.*
- *'At least you have another child.' Yes, and I love him fiercely and of course he brings me immense joy, but it doesn't make him a consolation prize.*
- *'How selfish.' NO NO NO. My son was a generous-hearted and sensitive, creative, complex soul. He was desperate and ill. His illness meant that he was not in control of his thoughts and actions. If anything, it was more likely that his thinking was so distorted he thought he was doing us a favour. And, of course, it makes me feel like a rubbish parent.*

- *'Time's a great healer.' It might be but the jury is definitely out and right now I don't have time. I need to know how to survive today.*

That's better.
XX

Just as some of our close friends don't know what to say to us, I now realise how little knowledge the professionals have about suicide. In between the despair that has taken over my entire existence both physical and mental, I have moments of crystalline clarity and pure rage at the unfairness of Dom's treatment. It is just not right and I have Cam's recent five-star cancer treatment to compare it to, which sharpens my gaze. I'm on a mission to understand Dom (which may never end) and in the process, I realise how the professionals tasked with helping him lacked the tools and knowledge to see how ill my boy was and how they failed to give me and Jan any useful support to keep him alive in our role as *de facto* carers. It makes me feel like a total fool not to have realised before how unfit for purpose our mental health system is. It's now – way too late – that I hear of the people who have paid to go to America or Europe to find the treatment they need. How could I be so in the dark? Bitterness is not my go-to medicine: it doesn't end well in my experience and I realise it's no one individual's fault. But we are years behind in our understanding of mental health. The stigma holds us back from investing in it, researching it, improving survival rates. The GP who sits on our sofa and asks how we are (good man) soaks it all up as I rant. It helps. I am finding some fuel to live on: the need for things to change.

Friends whose names are etched on my heart continue to live with us day and night. It's definitely not the glamorous good times of friendship. More in the vein of ironing, bin emptying and mouldy food disposal while doling out hugs and sharing tears and memories. They have seen parts of our marriage that most friends never witness, stopped us fraying apart. We have had no choice but to lean on them (the state has deserted us) and I'm pretty sure we would not be where we are without them. So many people are frightened of seeing others suffer but these guys have the courage to be our life raft. Once I can make a cup of tea – and even this small milestone takes weeks – they taper off the care plan and Jan and I start to spend time alone. They tell us that the upside is we have all started knocking on each other's doors again without an appointment and that this is what friendship is really all about. They reassure us they are in for the long haul.

Pat to Kerry
Hi Fish,

Completely understand that you can't come up yet – you are not a crap friend – you've got loads going on yourself! We're doing as well as can be expected. Our local friends are being AMAZING. Am totally humbled by how much they have put themselves out to keep us going. Dom's school have been incredibly supportive too. Never been more grateful to have a strong community around me. Xxx

One small goal, one breath at a time, we begin to find hope as we unsteadily follow a breadcrumb trail of kindness towards a new way of being.

How to be a good friend to someone in the darkest of times

We had each other and it was a lifeline. But we also needed friends who had a bit less on their own plate (or who lived nearby) and many of them stepped up over and over again. This is our chance to tip our hats in gratitude to them; it's not as easy as it looks.

- Let the person in pain say what they want to say – *I think he might die… I feel it's my fault… I should have…* – without jumping in to make things better, even if what you are hearing is uncomfortable. We weren't comforted by phrases like 'He'll be fine' because we knew it might not be true.
- Resist the temptation to say, 'Don't say things like that.' Firmly remind yourself that the person in pain is the one stuck with the situation and you only have to be in it with them for a while.
- Invite and persist – even if you get turned down more than once, try to squash the insecurity that you are not wanted. Don't take it personally if they aren't ready to be in a group or miss important celebrations such as birthdays. Row your boat towards them if they can't find their oars.

   Pat
   'Going through this massive crisis has made socialising more of a minefield. I used to thrive on it and still love seeing people but big groups can be overwhelming. Imagine what it would be like if you were introverted to start with. (P.S. I still want to be invited.)'

- In times of acute upset or stress, some people may not want or be able to leave their home because it feels like the one environment they can control. Be prepared to go to them rather than becoming fixated on getting them out and about. If they do not manage to leave the house, you might need to encourage them to see the GP or even go with them.
- If someone gives up work to care for a child, it doesn't mean they are suddenly available for days/lunches out. Serious illness is a hundred per cent time, energy and emotion consuming and often ties you to a home base.

Kerry

'Right in the middle of treatment, when we still didn't know if the chemo was working, one friend texted me to suggest that if I had 'nothing to do' I should go to a design exhibition she'd been to, to get some ideas for the new bathroom we'd been planning before Cam became ill. Although it was meant with good intentions, it just made me feel so isolated and lonely. It was as though she had no understanding at all of what it was like to be consumed with worry 24/7. I could barely think about what to cook for dinner, let alone have the headspace to look at tiles. New bathrooms belonged to another life.'

- Put yourself in their shoes. Group situations are hard because the chances are the friend in need feels like a big black crow at everyone's picnic. One-on-one or two is easier until everyone gets used to the horrible new normal.

Pat

'Constitutionals with the dog have become a very regular event with friends or our partners – gentle and intimate and as short or long as you want them to be.'

- It is great to say 'Let me know if I can do anything' but it's even better to be specific. For example, offer to walk the dog and state a time. Text when you're off to town and volunteer to run errands.

Kerry

'One friend took my Hoover away to be fixed. Another packaged up a new chair that had arrived broken and sorted out its return. Real helping isn't very glamorous.'

- Food is always very welcome. Send COOK vouchers if you don't know them well.
- If you do not live nearby, it can be harder to be practical but you can still stay in touch and be a listening ear.
- Think before you speak – it's human nature to want to put as much blue water as you can between someone else's tragedy and the possibility of it happening to you. But no one who has a child with cancer wants to hear about how you had a chart to tick off your kids' five-a-day fruit and veg or how they've never had a day without a fish oil/spirulina supplement (*subtext: unlike you, Kerry, my children are immune to cancer thanks to my excellent parenting skills*). And no one who has a suicidal child wants to be told that 'Johnny tells me everything. We're very close' (*subtext: you, Pat, were a bad parent and I am a good one*).
- It's a fine line between choosing your words carefully and becoming so tongue-tied that you're scared to get in touch, but if possible, try and avoid words/phrases such as 'heartbreaking', 'devastating', 'feels like the end of the world' when you're talking about everyday problems.
- Tread very carefully around comparisons: losing your beloved aunt, your dog, or anyone who has died at a ripe old

age can cause very deep and real grief, but does not compare to losing or fearing the loss of a child.

Pat

'When my dad was ill with heart failure, he comforted me by explaining that dying at his age (78) was sad but not tragic. It did not stop me grieving and feeling like I had been robbed when he died but it did help me understand a little of why it felt so vastly different when it was my child.'

- Don't suggest they read your friend's blog about cancer (or send a link without asking). Unless it's the actual cancer relating to their child (and maybe even then) it's unlikely they'll feel up to taking on anyone else's pain or good news story when their own resources are so stretched and the future is full of uncertainty. Similarly, be careful with the facts you include in any communication – don't include gloomy statistics/information that the parent might not know.

Kerry

'I'd deliberately avoided googling Grey Zone lymphoma and one friend, who was being really kind and helpful, managed to send an email letting me know it was a "rare and aggressive cancer".'

- Conversely, if you do happen to be an expert in something or have any useful contacts now is absolutely the right time to offer them up.

Pat

'The best advice, if you are at all worried, is to ask someone directly whether they are considering suicide. The thought

that someone might have known that, and didn't tell me, is unbearable.'

- Almost anything is better than nothing if it's well intentioned but here are the really useful things to say: 'That sounds very tough.' 'I'm so sorry to hear what's happened.' 'How are you feeling right now?' 'How can I help?' The standard 'How are you?' also works as long as you are prepared for an expletive-filled response.
- Even if you are friends with both parents, it might be a good idea to see them separately now and again. Everyone copes in different ways and it can be a relief to speak openly without having to protect a partner. In our experience, the men need as much support as the women, but find it harder to start the conversation. Be brave.
- Push a note through the front door even if you've texted to say you're going to leave a package/food in the shed/behind the bins and so on. We found our brains didn't hold peripheral information very well when we were in the depths of trauma.

Kerry
'Even though my lovely friend had said she was making a lasagne and would leave it in the shed, I completely forgot and found it a week later – ugh! Similarly, I got a beautiful fruit parcel but the note was missing and I drove myself mad feeling so rude because I couldn't thank the sender and was really grateful when she asked me whether it had arrived.'

Pat
'Here are some ideas for positive postcards that you can stick around your home or stuff in the front of your diary. They might not work for everyone but they worked for me. Obviously you can also find your own.'

If you can be one thing, be kind.

Invest in friendships. Love is all there is in the end.

Find your 3 a.m. friends – the ones you can call on in a crisis – and keep them close.

If you cannot pay an act of friendship back, pay it forwards.

A friend is: someone who can look you in the eye, see your pain and stay by your side.

Real friends don't mind doing the ironing.

CHAPTER TWENTY-FOUR

Pat

Held Together by Love

Mid-November

The days continue to merge. A fraction more bearable than the restless nights. I long for sleep and dread its arrival. Sleep is where the deeper griefs dwell: unwanted flashes of memory, back to my last moments with Dom and all the 'what ifs' that come with them. And deeper still. Dark scenes I cannot stop imagining of Dom's last moments alone.

I find a Buddhist meditation on suicide loss on Google and read it every day at least once and often more. It gives me a framework for holding my thoughts and turning them towards goodwill, peace and acceptance. It starts to bring the fullness of Dom back to the foreground, reducing the dreadful power of the way he died... *I know that suffering and confusion are not your essence... You love me and I love you.*

But I still long for a sign of life from beyond. The beginning of each new day arrives with the crushing reality of Dom's death. One night I am rewarded with a vivid image of Dom standing in the bedroom doorway, smiling and haloed in golden light. I wake weeping and choose to take the sign as a blessing.

Visitors pop in (there must surely be text-based coordination going on behind the scenes). I make tiny steps to the outside world: walking the dog in the dark so no one can see me and a trip to the same garden centre I frequented with Dom, my arm gripped tight by the friend who takes me there as I teeter on the edge of a full panic attack but manage to hold it at bay.

The funeral date has been set for 22 November. It gives us time to reflect a little rather than hurtling through without a pause. It's not as if it changes anything. The deadline is long since passed for that. Neil, who has agreed to lead the home-made service, spends evenings at the kitchen table with us and we often walk and talk through the possible plans and what we might say. Dom has left recordings of his repertoire of songs on the iPad. Jan and I cannot bear to watch the videos together as the emotions run too wild for us to contain but we manage in Neil's company and look into Dom's eyes as he performs to the camera with our kitchen cupboards in view behind him. We all sob out our love; the familiar words to 'Titanium' and 'Thank You for the Music' carry an altogether different weight when viewed from this new perspective. I don't think I will ever hear these lyrics again without seeing Dom's face and hearing the loneliness in his voice. Gradually the funeral takes shape and Jan, Greg and I all agree that we will try to speak about our love for Dom. We hope it might help us come to terms with what's happened. For me, it is something I feel I must do to honour my love for him. But it is hard hard yards to find the right words.

Pat to Kerry
Sorry for radio silence, Fish, we've had gastric flu cos that's what you need when this happens and you are meeting with the funeral people yippeeee NOT. Love you. xxxx

Kerry to Pat
Oh no! Hang on in there. Thinking about you all the time.
Such a tough week ahead. We're there for you next week
and beyond. Sending lots of love your way. xx

Pat to Kerry
Thanks Fish. We're making the best of the cards we've been
dealt. Up and down like squally weather but unbelievably,
moments of serenity and laughter too. Cannot wait to see
you. Hope Cam is okay too. See you Tuesday night? xxx

Jan and I arrange to meet the funeral director at the hotel chapel where we have chosen to remember Dom's life and say goodbye to him. The hotel is a place that means a lot to us. We have been there for so many Mother's Day lunches, Christmas and birthday meals over the years that the staff know us well. We feel safe and are sure Dom would approve.

The funeral director sits opposite us in dark attire softened by a kindly face. It's incongruous to be in such a smart, business-like room with fancy biscuits on the table discussing coffins for my son. It's completely beyond anything I have ever imagined doing in my lifetime. As new parents, full of love and wonder, no one sets out thinking that this is where it ends. I would never have thought myself capable of it and yet here I am, leafing obediently through the catalogue. On the unstable edge of sanity and with a violent and inexplicable rejection of anything too solid, too earthed, I suggest cardboard, thinking about Dom's love of all things eco. The funeral director makes a note, fiddles with his pen and looks over my left ear as he searches for the words to explain that it might not be the most robust choice given the rainy autumn weather and our wish to carry the coffin ourselves. He pauses for a moment to let that sink in and then turns the page in the brochure. 'Perhaps bamboo would be a good compromise?'

I eventually grasp what he is trying to say and of course he is right. The thought of soggy cardboard goes beyond even my dark humour boundaries. 'That's the one,' I say, tapping the pale bamboo coffin in the picture and looking to Jan, who nods his agreement. With visible relief, flushed with the strain of trying to avoid explaining the science of what happens when water and cardboard make contact, the undertaker writes down the details. Another of the many decisions on the road to the funeral is made. It feels like something Dom would like. A natural material for this most unnatural order of things event.

As we pull onto the drive in winter darkness after a gruelling afternoon, we are greeted by a husband on delivery duty who hands over a bag and bottle of wine, gives me a warm hug and scurries off, not wanting to disturb. Food thoughtfully prepared by his wife. It's completely unexpected and way after the first flurry of lasagnes have been eaten. These acts of kindness come when we least expect them and need them most. Jan and I tuck into mushroom and tarragon tagliatelle washed down with a bottle of something red.

Greg wants to fly in on the morning of the funeral and my adrenaline hits the roof at the thought of such tight timing. We manage to persuade him to come earlier, to get his bearings before the day. His friends have offered to come with him and we're delighted; it means we'll have a house full of life-giving energy. He's blessed to have such kind, loyal friends from school and college. It's a lot to ask of carefree youth to spend time in the presence of death.

One day, in the week before the funeral, I find the courage to take a huge pile of cards upstairs and sit on the bed feeling the weight of them in my hands. They have been left untouched since we came back from Cornwall. We knew they were there, full of support and sorrow but neither of us had the strength to open them, to touch the grief they might release. Now I need to work out if there is anyone else who needs to know about the funeral, so I start to read. So many people, all fumbling for the right words to reach us. Although I can barely see the writing through a wash of tears, I imagine each one as part of an invisible net of love wrapped around us, holding us together when we cannot do it for ourselves.

Gradually the words and pictures that frame the service come together. We will celebrate Dom's life and talents. A dear artist friend who's known Dom since birth uses his artwork, some of her own, words from him and me to pull together something for us to give to everyone at the funeral. We don't even know what to call it. Is it a programme? Order of Service is the traditional name but it does not seem adequate for this reflection on who Dom was and what he means to us. It's a work of art in its own right. Although it's one of the hardest things I've ever done, this process helps me to absorb some of Dom into my being. It's intensely personal. There is no room for strangers in this intimate send-off.

Jan, Greg, Neil and I write about Dom and share our tributes with each other. We read them to ourselves and shed tears in private and then we stumble through them together. To give us a fighting chance of surviving the day to come, everyone practises until the feelings become more controllable. Gradually, as we speak our heart words we falter less and find our flow. We do it for Dom, out of our love for him.

CHAPTER TWENTY-FIVE

Pat

In Gratitude

20–21 November

Kerry to Pat
We'll grab a cab and come over when we arrive but happy to let a restaurant take the strain if you're up to going out. I am embarrassed that I have so little idea about what you can cope with/what feels appropriate. Hopefully I'll have a better understanding once we've got together. xx

Pat to Kerry
We're doing as okay as you could possibly expect all things considered. Still laughing (just) but now with buckets of engulfing loss and tears. See you tomorrow. I'm baking scones in the afternoon to Dom's recipe with the hotel chef for Dom's Gathering (it's what we are calling the wake after the funeral) then supper here and we're playing it by ear.

Tuesday 21 November

On the eve of Dom's funeral, Neil drives me, Jan and Greg to the chapel in a rehearsal of what we will do for real the next day. Each of us chooses a pew and sits for a while wrapped in our private thoughts, sensing the space settle peacefully around us, musty notes of incense seeping from the woodwork. Neil gently steers us as we each take a turn to speak with the microphone. The words hit us afresh, even though we have practised. Greg is crushed with sorrow when he speaks out to the empty pews. We keep each other steady, hold each other until we feel strong enough to carry on.

The chapel and the 'Not Altar', as we have nicknamed it, look beautiful. They've been decorated lovingly by friends: live succulents, silk flowers (cut flowers made Dom sad) and his favourite candles.

Friends and family spend the evening with us and bring hearty fish pie (it's become a staple). Their chatter keeps our minds on the moment rather than being sucked into either the past or the future, neither of which are places we want to go right now. Greg and his friends are filling the house with the welcome bustle that comes from so many people taking turns for the shower and hunting for their shoes in the pile by the door (I'd never have guessed how, one day, I would be glad to trip over huge teenage trainers).

CHAPTER TWENTY-SIX

Kerry

Surreal Yet Real

21 November 2017

We arrive in Harrogate the night before Dom's funeral. It feels surreal; last time we were here was May, before our lives all imploded, when our greatest worries were which restaurant to choose and whether the white wine was cold enough. Now Dom is dead, that little boy I remember from our holiday together in Ireland, carefully choosing a sad-eyed puppy in a little pottery shop, making blackberry and apple crumble with a precise view about the topping, horse-riding along Rossbeigh beach on the Wild Atlantic Way. At the same time, I struggle to focus on the enormity of why we are actually here because my own heart is stretching back to Surrey. It's the first time we've left Cam without one of us and although he's in good hands, with my dad and step-mum and friends, I keep checking my phone. I don't know if we're being irresponsible, passing the burden to other people to make a judgement call about whether Cam needs to go to hospital if his temperature spikes. I've taught Michaela how to inject him with Filgrastim and I trust her, but again, it seems like a huge ask.

But we couldn't not come.

The night we arrive, along with some of their close friends, we have dinner with Pat and Jan at their home – and I'm struck by their strength. It's still so good to see them, to be able to hug them tightly, which somehow conveys so much more love than any text or email could ever express. It's just over three months since Pat came on her mercy mission to join me in hospital when Cam was first diagnosed. Three short months in which she's lost her son and we're clinging on to the hope that we'll keep ours. The picture that keeps pinging into my head is the summer after we graduated nearly thirty years ago when we hung out at the beach, windsurfing and playing cards, excited about the next stage of our lives, with Pat starting a job in marketing and me heading off to Spain to teach English. I wish we could run back to that sweet spot in time, to that certainty that life only held good things for us.

But we've got no choice but to get on with the hand that life has dealt us. I've never been really close to anyone who's experienced such tragedy before – and I'm relieved to see that despite the huge sadness in Pat and Jan, there's no awkwardness between us: we're all the rawest we've ever been but we're still capable of laughing together. It feels a bit odd to be meeting the few friends we haven't come across before in such unusual circumstances; we're all tiptoeing about, not quite sure of the etiquette for superficial 'Do you live in Harrogate?/Such a lovely town/We're staying at the Hotel du Vin' chit-chat in the shadow of tomorrow's events. It's almost worse with the ones we've bumped into before at joyous celebrations – weddings, christenings and big birthday dos – but don't know very well. We flail around for the appropriate meet and greet after so many years when we're all so sad. The conversation inevitably falls onto the familiar territory that unites so many people: 'And how are your children? What are they up to?' I see the questions heading my way, shrink back from them, but cannot avoid them. I feel a sense of guilt at adding more gloom to an occasion already steeped in desperation, but our reality is so fresh, I don't have the dexterity of thought required to lie.

Thankfully Greg is here with some of his friends from university; their youthful exuberance isn't dimmed by our solemnity. They're still laughing and joking about, unabashed. We could learn a lot from them, especially from the girl who offers to sleep in Dom's room – 'It has a peaceful vibe.'

CHAPTER TWENTY-SEVEN

Pat

How Can This Be Goodbye?

22 November 2017

The palms of my hands are pressed against the edge of the sink; I am leaning against it as the waves of dizziness swirl through. Looking in the mirror, face masked in make-up and waterproof mascara, I feel betrayed that I do not look as ravaged as I feel. If the outside looked like the inside, I would be a balding, snivelling and wrinkled old crone.

I have mentally prepared myself for this because I want to feel present on the day, not washed away by it. Over and again, I have visualised a meticulous plan of the routine that I will go through to take me from waking to sunset on the day of my Dom's funeral.

Just as for a wedding, only absolutely devastatingly not, we are the last to leave the house. We squeeze into Neil's car. I'll never get to choose a hat for the big gay wedding now. In crisp air, golden light catching the autumn leaves, we look towards the oak-carved doors of the chapel, collecting ourselves. The insides of my cheeks are shredded from constant biting and I am numb, frozen from the heart outwards, and stiff from the effort of not collapsing. We hide away in the hotel with a plate of untouched sandwiches because none of us can bear the strain of meeting anyone beforehand. As the bell tolls the hour, we stand outside the side door of the chapel in semi-darkness. We lean into each other, hands are squeezed and, holding our heads high for Dom, we pass in front of the Not Altar towards our reserved front-row seats. The ones no one wants to be in at any funeral, let alone one like this. I catch my sisters' eyes as we walk in and register that the chapel is packed but I face resolutely forwards, only pausing to place my hand on Dom's coffin. Silently, I tell him I love him to Pluto and back a million times.

I have my index finger on the diazepam tucked in my pocket. Emergency rations in case I cannot make it through. I've barely used any since we came home but I only last until I hear Dom's voice fill the chapel with 'How Would You Feel?' by Ed Sheeran before I snap it in two and slip half under my tongue. At least this way I can stay physically in the room and am glad to find I am mostly able to take it in as Dom's friends, Greg, Jan and Neil speak. I am so proud of them all. But the words, the lyrics, Dom's eyes, his lopsided smile and dimple whip up a whirlwind of grief and the sensation of living in the wrong universe on the wrong path sweeps my shattered soul to the sky. Huddled on this lonely front bench, our family feels pitifully small. My knuckles are white as I cling on to the wooden rail in front of me. Feeling the wall of love at my back in this chapel gives me just enough of a lifeline to inhale air. I try to imagine each of these people sharing the load so that we may bear what we must bear.

Gazing out from the lectern across the sea of so many familiar faces, I wonder if I will find a voice but I focus on my notes. In bright red capitals they say: A Mother's Love 22 November 2017. *Breathe… Do Dom justice… Smile.*

And I talk about how he knew we loved him and he loved us. The gifts he gave me of patience, living in the moment and gratitude for all that we have had. I dare to talk of when he came out as gay and the bullying that followed, how it taught me that kindness, a live and let live approach to all our fellow beings is really the only way to create a decent world to live in. I speak out loud my mother love for him, how I wish I had known how to stop him slipping through my fingers. It's way way too late but I hope he can hear me.

And afterwards, when the last echoes of his heartbreaking recording of 'Fools Rush In' have faded away, I stand with my husband, son and brother, and I rest a corner of the bamboo coffin on my shoulder. The sound of Bob Chilcott's 'Irish Blessing' fills the chapel as I embrace the weight of Dom's body for one last time and we carry him out.

CHAPTER TWENTY-EIGHT

Kerry

In Absolute Awe

22 November 2017

On the morning of the funeral, I'm oddly numb as though what is about to happen is so utterly devastating that I cannot allow myself to crack open the door to any emotion, in case I get washed away. Steve is charged with directing friends and family to their allotted places. In an attempt to keep my feelings under control, I concentrate on the other mourners. The church is packed beyond capacity and Steve valiantly directs latecomers, urging people to shuffle up to make room for older members of the congregation to sit down. Right now, I'm glad Pat's mum and dad are no longer alive, that they've been spared having to attend the funeral of their grandson.

With great effort, I stand dry-eyed while Jan, Greg and Dom's friends speak about him. Their eulogies are interspersed with videos of him singing, which is both uplifting and eerie, and underlines their loss so spectacularly. How can this boy who deliberately left these films for his parents to find, who does such a Dom/teenage thing of presenting his best side to the camera, making us all smile as he fusses with his hair, have really believed that the world was better off without him? I try to fathom it out but it feels like grappling with something huge that I don't have the brain capacity to understand, like how the stars sit in the sky or how countries don't fall off a round world. And in between my thoughts are full of the absolute admiration I have for Jan and Greg, that they can hold themselves together long enough to tell us what they want to share about Dom. I have flashes of fear that this is a dress rehearsal for us. I feel selfish and small, almost heartless, for even thinking about our situation but I can't help it.

My eyes flick over the message on the order of service.

A message from Dom's family...

Dom would have preferred to be here with us right now living his life to the full and sharing all of his talents and love with us. We know that because, among other things, he had written his Christmas list, his aspirations for a happy life and was looking forward to seeing our new bulbs we planted come up in spring. He was planning to go either to uni or take a gap year.

So, although he is peaceful now and his spirit is free, please do not think that this is what he wanted for himself. His illness got the better of him and in his healthy mind he would have much preferred to be here right now, sharing all of his favourite songs with us, being with his friends and loving his family; living life to the full.

It will help us enormously if all of you would please now go on to live your lives to the fullest after we have celebrated our beautiful boy, Dom, here today.   *Rest Easy Dom*

I don't think I've ever respected anyone more in my life when Pat gets up and talks about Dom. Her words are infused with that peculiar brand of maternal love – fierce, defiant and unconditional – without ever straying into the territory of making out he was perfect. My mind struggles to accept what I am seeing, that my friend is speaking at *her son's funeral*. I love her for taking the opportunity to make sure we understand that Dom's suicide isn't the thing that defines him – although that was the devastating outcome of his diseased mind – but that he was so many other joyful things besides: an artist, baker, singer, saxophonist, good friend and listening ear. I have to keep reminding myself that she isn't giving a speech at his birthday, that she is actually doing the thing that no mother should ever have to do.

The simplicity and futility of hearing her say, 'I wish I could hold his hand and tell him again how much I love him but it comforts me to know that he knew I did. I wish I'd known how to stop him slipping through my fingers but it comforts me to know he's free and at peace and wants us to live our lives joyfully,' breaks through the steel doors I've erected around my heart. I cling to Steve's arm, sobbing, as she dips her shoulder under Dom's coffin, and with Jan, Greg and Pat's brother, takes Dom on a journey none of them ever wanted to make.

CHAPTER TWENTY-NINE

Kerry

Staggering On

End of November–Mid-December 2017

Pat to Kerry
Hi Fish

Feel like I didn't get enough time to talk this week but so glad you were there. Greg is going back to Cornwall today and I'm resisting the urge to fasten a tagging device to his ankle. We've had a few good meals the three of us since his friends left. Very sad but we're also laughing… funny old time. How's Cam doing?

Kerry to Pat
Hi Patti

Must be hellish waving Greg off. Thinking about you so much. Cam has a stinking cold so chemo on 30 Nov is in the balance. Ho hum.

Pat to Kerry
Oh Fish, Hope Cam's cold is going away. It's shit and scary for you guys I know and please, please don't stop talking to

me about it. I want to help and be there for you and will
still make you laugh I promise!

As November stumbles to a close, the good news that the tumour has shrunk dramatically appears to have had a detrimental effect on our stability. I can't help feeling it's because we're too scared to hope in case it's snatched away from us again, but Cam in particular is more despondent than I've ever seen him. He's starting to fall behind at school. He can't concentrate (chemo can lead to muddled thinking) and the cumulative effects of the treatment are catching up with him. We discuss him repeating the year. I'm in two minds: I'm way past caring about A-level grades but I want him to keep looking forwards. School gives him a routine and us all a valuable breathing space from focusing relentlessly on cancer. It feels utterly unrealistic but I don't want him to just give up, for this bloody disease to hold him back, to derail the life plan he had. It will be so hard for him to watch all his peers heading off on new adventures at university next autumn while he hangs back with the year below. He shows no enthusiasm for sorting out his UCAS forms but he agrees to apply to study business. He gets quite aggressive about not wanting to 'play the cancer card' in his personal statement. My view is that there has to be *some* upside to his bad luck.

In the end, he manages his own unique twist on it, saying that he's had the unfortunate experience of witnessing first-hand the challenges that face a huge organisation like the NHS in delivering a quality service on a large scale. I phone all the universities to find out how much flexibility there is regarding the grades offered, as I don't want to set Cam up for a disappointment. If he does get some A-levels, I want him to celebrate, not feel that he's failed. Only one person I speak to in admissions acknowledges what I've said with an 'Oh my God, you poor things.' The rest direct me robot-like towards the mitigating circumstances on their websites as though I'm somehow trying to cheat the system.

We blunder through the beginning of winter, sustained by a core band of friends who seem to be doing a grand job of fighting off compassion fatigue. The local ones drop round with wine, food and flowers; the ones who live further away stay for the weekend, bringing their stories from the outside world, making us laugh despite ourselves. One lovely woman whom I only know from dog walking on the hill regularly leaves a parcel of home-baked cakes or cookies on my doorstep. These little acts of kindness lift my heart.

The day before Cam's next chemo my new book, *The Secret Child*, is being released. I haven't worked at all since he became ill. I feel guilty but I can't concentrate, can't write a word, certainly nothing that requires imagination. The reality of life seems to have sucked out every little bit of oxygen from the part of my brain required to invent people, lives, *solutions*. My lovely editor has taken all the work away from me, the various stages of the editing process sorted out in-house. I recognise how lucky I am compared to the poor parents I see tapping away on their laptops while poison is pumped into their kids, pressed up against the windows at odd angles in desperation for a mobile phone signal. The night before publication I force myself to make a promotional video. Michaela films me. At the end of the excerpt, I read out the dedication at the front of the book – 'To Cam and all the other teenage boys out there who probably have absolutely no idea how much they are loved' – and feel my voice catch. I'd written it before he got ill and on really dark days wonder if I'd had a premonition, or worse, had somehow 'made it happen' by writing that, even though the old me would have thought I was an absolute idiot for even allowing that idea headspace. In the video, I look fine, calm, maybe more serious than usual. No one would know how heavy my heart is.

The next day, Cam is well enough for chemo despite looking so thin and pale. I try to keep in mind the progress we've made, telling myself that it's the treatment that's making him ill not the cancer, but controlling my fear is a battle I'm in danger of losing. Thankfully, an old friend, Kate, is visiting London from Canada and offers to come and sit with me while Cam sleeps through his chemo. It seems a terrible waste of a day's holiday but she insists and I'm so grateful to have a distraction. Her mother has advanced dementia and she's no stranger to hospitals. While the chemo clicks through, we laugh, catch up on news and occasionally stop to marvel that the twenty-somethings who worked together in Florence, squeaking into the office straight from a weekend at the beach, have become these careworn people.

We stagger towards Christmas. Michaela makes me dye my hair; in fact, buys the dye for me and puts it on. I think the grey frightens her, a physical manifestation of my ageing when she needs to be sure I'm going to be around to help her through this. I try desperately to find some Christmas cheer but don't have the energy to trail around looking for inspiration. I hate shopping at the best of times and somehow, throwing money at stuff we don't need seems particularly obscene this year. The only thing I want, probably the only thing I'll ever want again, money can't buy. I'm also not strong enough to go into town and risk bumping into people I know. I can't answer questions about what we're doing for Christmas, when the next chemo on 21 December is blotting out everything else.

Michaela takes over and orders gifts for Steve and Cam. I don't even know what she's buying and I can't find it in myself to care. I force myself to do one big shop for Michaela – even in my super-advanced humbug state I can't expect her to buy her own presents. We dig deep, drag the Christmas tree out of the garage and Michaela and I decorate it. Everything takes on a new poignancy: the salt dough stars they made in primary school, the funny felt Father Christmases, their glitter long gone. I can't even remember who made what and a year ago I'd have probably been tempted to wang the whole lot into the bin, only hanging on to them because it's easier to shove them back in the box every year than to take a few minutes to sort through them. Suddenly, though, these decorations have become precious, a reminder of an innocent time when we had no idea what was in store. I've never been sentimental about stuff like that and I'm irritated by myself. I don't want to become that person who has to cling on to every bit of the past they've never appreciated before. But I fear I might.

Please don't let this be my last Christmas with Cam.

Pat to Kerry
We're doing okay generally… managing to be kind most of the time and trying to do something we enjoy each day. Trying to avoid what ifs and mother guilt is the tricky bit for me so just occasionally I fall into that bear pit and have to drag myself back out… Has Cam decided whether to do his exams yet? Often think about you – know you're dealing with deep ongoing shit too.

Kerry to Pat
I think you've done amazingly well not to fall into the bear pit more often. Motherhood is so often about guilt. I worry all the time now in a way I didn't before. Cami is going to do his mocks, then we'll go from there. I feel I can't take anything for granted, the optimism with which I breezed through life is severely dented and I don't know who I am any more. I look forward to finding a piece of the old me one day! The old us in fact. I'm sure carefree times will come for us both again but God I'm getting impatient.

Pat to Kerry
It's all so grown up, isn't it? Love you, Fish. You're still you, feisty strong woman with powerful lioness instincts – and still laughing (most of the time!).

Taming guilt – Kerry

Guilt is a huge issue, partly because motherhood is already rife with 'shoulda/woulda/coulda' and there aren't many prizes for getting it right, just jeers for getting it wrong. But when I dig down into my specific guilt around Cam's illness, I find several recurring themes.

There's the obvious one of packing him off on rugby tour with a cough but I've managed to forgive myself for that because I don't think there are too many mothers who would go 'tickly cough equals lymphoma'. Next on the pile is that I didn't give Michaela the attention she needed and because she's a coper, resilient and resourceful, I assumed that she was doing okay. In the early days of Cam's diagnosis, I knew she'd be at home a lot on her own as it was the summer holidays. Steve and I were spending large chunks of time at the hospital and I wanted to spare her the gruelling reality of sitting around the ward. I arranged for her to stay with my mum and, later, some friends. Looking back, I think she felt shut out. I also worry I was hotwiring her brain to believe that the only person in the family who was important was Cam.

For much of the time, on the surface of it, Michaela's life carried on relatively normally, albeit with a massive axe hanging above us on a fraying rope. She was going to school, as was Cam, so we still had people to stay, went out for dinner as a family, walked to the cafe with the dog. I have videos of Cam and Chaela singing to his music in the car seemingly without a care in the world (making sure to shout out all the swear words to annoy me).

I've been relieved to see scrolling back that I took pictures of Michaela on my phone during that period, as well as photos of clothes she might like for Christmas, so maybe it's not as black and white as my memory now records it. What I know I didn't do well, though, was consciously make time to take her out on her own and really listen to her. Because my main focus was on getting from chemo to chemo, I didn't stop often enough to say, 'Are you really okay or just pretending to be because you know we've got so much worry already?' Neither did I understand that it was important to her for me not to talk about Cam when they were her 'occasions' – parents' evening, dental appointments, picking her up from parties. I hope to make up for that in the coming years.

Next on the list are the flashbacks to the times when I wasn't very kind to Cam – or anyone – because fear and worry had exhausted me. His desire to party, socialise, stay out late never abated, taking me to the very edge of insanity. He often finished six or seven hours of chemo and went straight out with his friends, with me standing at the door shouting after him to take his antibiotics. It was such a difficult balance between his 'I might die, Mum, so at least let me live now' and my need to keep him at home to feed him kale and cabbage, washed down with a glass of pomegranate juice. More than once the fear that he'd wear himself out and become too ill for chemo led to me bellowing things at him that were so unpleasant I cannot write them here because my shame is so great.

Before Cam was ill, I assumed that anyone in my situation would somehow become super-patient and loving and make the most of every moment. But in reality, I was already dealing with the challenges of the teenage years, with all the impulsiveness and lack of awareness of danger that entails. And that was before I even started to unpick the mindset of a boy who didn't know whether he'd make his eighteenth birthday. I wasn't facing these issues after I'd just popped back refreshed from a long holiday in the Caribbean; I was dealing with them after weeks of sleepless nights, after excruciating hours in A&E waiting to see if an infection was the result of the cancer spreading, after months of the roller-coaster ups and downs of serious illness.

So if you're reading this, entirely ashamed that you've just blown up at a child with whom you would gladly swap places and die tomorrow in their stead, be kind to yourself. You are human and long-term illness is relentless in its eating up of endurance and resilience. My behaviour never came about because I didn't love him, it came about because I feared losing him.

I wish I'd found a way to sit calmly and explain that.

Taming guilt – Pat

Guilt is the mighty warrior of misery against which I battle on a daily basis. It lurks in the huge tangled mess of my own conscience telling me I should or could have done differently. And it is also there in an imagined and unforgiving public jury passing sentence on the parenting decisions I've taken. All of which is perched on top of the mountain of guilt that seems to come with the package of being a mum. Every thread that I pick at unravels to the same pointless place: a riddle that I will never solve.

If Dom had recovered from his illness, I may not have had the same urge to scour my heart or look for the wrong turnings. Now, it physically pains me to hear other parents measure their prowess by the accomplishments of their children. If they can take all the credit for success then I, in turn, must surely take all the blame for failure?

But I have come to realise that I am not all powerful, much as I would like to have been. On a bad day, I feel as if I have fallen at the first hurdle of parenting – actually keeping my child alive. On a good day, I also know that I did everything that I could to keep him here with us. My very first counsellor made me write an affirmation about guilt after a long time talking about it: *I always do my very best.* For months, I could not recognise it as something that would be true of me but I am working on it – occasionally I say it and even believe it.

Another wise woman suggested that I see taming the guilt as 'work in progress' so that I don't have to wait for full absolution (from myself).

There is also the ongoing guilt of letting others down – Dom foremost and forever but also the families and colleagues at school, friends and neighbours who sent cards and messages which were read but not replied to, the countless invites to meet for a coffee which were forgotten in the brain fog that death left behind. I can't shake the feeling that people think I'm rude and ungrateful.

Fighting off the thoughts that spiral to guilt feels like teetering on the edge of an inky black whirlpool. Because I know it could wash me away, I apply a huge amount of willpower to direct my thoughts in a more useful direction. This exhausts me to a degree I would never have understood before. I've gathered knowledge to fend off the worst of the self-hatred. I've tried to learn as much as I can about mental health, suicide, trauma and attachment to make some sense of what has happened. It helps but I also know that, whatever I learn, I will never know for sure if I am creating a version of the truth to protect myself. I know that the one thing I want will never be possible, which is to ask Dom directly.

As a form of confession, I have needed to say aloud my worst fears about being a bad mother. In particular, I had to articulate these emotions to my closest friends to check they wouldn't reject me if they knew what I really thought. In the first year, I said it to anyone who would listen: to counsellors, mentors, strangers I met on trains. I told them that I thought I had made mistakes. I was lucky enough to avoid the harsh judgement that many who lose a child to suicide experience and it helped me greatly to have my feelings accepted rather than denied. I'm trying to show the same compassion to my former self as others have. I think it might be a lifetime's work.

CHAPTER THIRTY

Pat

Who Am I Now?

Late November and the run-up to Christmas 2017

I crawl through the time after Dom's Gathering in a state of flat-battery exhaustion. My waking thoughts are consumed by Dom: his elegant hands playing the piano, his voice, that giggle, his annoying habits that I would give anything to be annoyed by again, the last moments we shared and the words he spoke. The dark mornings make it easy to stay in bed until the blackbird's song breaks the silence. Propped up on pillows, I meditate using a script about coming to terms with suicide loss. Next, allowing no time for a relapse, I count in my head: three, two, one and swing my legs to the floor. Restocking the bird feeder and breathing are the points of focus that give me a tiny framework to live by. I cry endlessly, tears with such intensity that I have to stop and lean on the worktop, door frame or nearest tree, hugging myself until they recede. If someone who loves me is nearby (or even almost strangers on occasion) they can hold me. It is all they can do and sometimes I can't even bear that. Writing my journal lays the foundations of my survival plan. Maybe it will act as a sluice gate to control the emotions pressing against the dam of fear. Maybe writing will stop me being swept away. I fold inwards; the world beyond pain barely registers.

Thursday 30 November

Telling my life story, Dom's death story, to the counsellor with no filters about the response makes me feel liberated. I often feel as if I am qualifying my reactions, judging them with imagined external eyes. Why do I feel as if there is a 'right way' to do this? What is *this*? I came away from that first appointment with an instruction to keep a daily journal noting my feelings and something of beauty in nature. I remember the barely used pink A4 lined school notebook I found when I was tidying Dom's room. Stroking the pens he too must have held, I carefully choose one and leave his neat handwritten notes about social influence from his A-level Psychology lesson intertwined with my own ramblings.

Counselling session one:

1. Accept that the letting go is the greatest act of love.
2. Who am I now?
3. How do I synthesise doing and being?
4. Meditate for twenty minutes each day.
5. Keep walking and noticing nature.

Because I crave some structure in these formless days, the instruction to walk the dog and notice nature really does help. I make myself go out every day, rain or shine. One afternoon it begins to snow, the wet, unwelcome kind. It brings with it a disorienting panic that the world is moving away from me while I am stranded – bewildered in the wake of destruction.

Pat to Kerry
Hi Fish

Moods all over the place, changing faster than the weather. Bloody nightmare really – so much pent-up trauma. Completely random crying. All hideous. Jan and I are okay but it gets very rocky when we both crash – then we cling on by our fingernails until it passes over. x

Kerry to Pat
Oh bless you both. I won't bore you with everything going on here. Dare I ask if you've made a decision about work? Big love. xxx

Pat to Kerry
I've asked work for the rest of this school year to give me time to think. No plan B if they say no. I'm not ready for the outside world yet. xx

Retreat, Restore, Relaunch is the new mantra by which I live my days. The warmth of my counsellor, who has heard it all without flinching, provides enough safety for me to formulate a plan. These three words reassure me that there might be a way through this. They also help me explain what I mean when I tell others I am doing grief work.

Richard, a fellow headteacher, is sitting on my sofa with Caragh leaping all over him, shedding hair. I can tell he's being polite as he brushes ineffectually at his suit and says it's alright but I take him at his word, knowing she will settle protectively next to me once the novelty is over. I'm so grateful to him for being brave enough to visit. He and Neil together have been above and beyond in their response. Richard tells me how missed I will be if I don't go back to teaching, get back in the saddle. He's very persuasive but luckily for me he fell off his own bike and broke his ribs recently. I use this to explain that, having been a back-on-your-bike person all my life, this is different. This may break me if I don't take it seriously now. I describe how I can hold a public face for a while but it cracks when I least expect it. And, of course, it terrifies me to reveal this truth to a professional friend but I take a gamble that I can trust him.

My confidence is shattered on all fronts so being told that I am needed and valued is priceless and I slot the feelings it brings into my inner piggy bank for later. We get to talking about Dom and I air my views on mental health and what schools could do to help. Richard interrupts just as I am hitting my stride to ask if I would like to speak at the summer teachers' conference. I leap on the offer. A life raft that is far enough away to be possible but near enough to feel real. Something to aim for.

Not a single day passes without a message or knock on the door. Friends and family from near and far, some reconnecting after a long gap, weave a protective cocoon while we start out on the long road to healing. I take constitutionals, sometimes needing to be pressed into walking and talking as I try to make sense of the incomprehensible. How could someone who loved life so much feel so desperate that this seemed like a good idea? What did I miss? What could I have done differently? I search for the turn in the road that leads to the future I dreamt of, the one he talked of himself: art school or university, living in London. I know he loved me and that he knew I loved him. It's bitterly tough to accept that wasn't enough in the face of a complex mental illness. Although I torture the questions, no answers come. Yet without fail I feel a bit better after each walk.

The embers left by the lack of answers flare into a passion to change the future and save others. The system needs a rewrite on the premise that suicide is preventable, not something that we have to hide from. The idea that 'if they are going to do it you can't stop them' needs shredding along with all the other paralysing myths.

Debunking myths

Myth: Talking about suicide might give someone the idea.

Reality: Talking directly about suicide in a responsible way (see papyrus-uk.org or zerosuicidealliance.com for examples) makes it less likely to happen.

Myth: People who talk about suicide are not serious and won't go through with it.

Reality: People who kill themselves have often told someone that they do not feel that life is worth living or that they have no future. They may even have said that they want to die. It is important to always take someone seriously if they talk about dying or feeling suicidal.

Myth: People who are suicidal want to die.

Reality: Most people who are suicidal do not want to die but they do not want to live the life they have at that moment in time. It may be that they cannot see how to change it, but with support can find solutions.

Being brave might save a life in these circumstances because all the research shows if you get it out in the open then the other person feels safer to talk about their feelings. Ask directly. For example: 'You seem very low. I am worried about you. Are you thinking of suicide/taking your own life?'

No one ever told me this so I forgive myself (most of the time) but please, never say, as I did, 'You're not going to do anything stupid/silly are you?' because a) in an ill mind it might not seem stupid, it might be the only option the person can see, and b) it is a highly judgemental phrase that might put someone off talking to you about suicidal thoughts in the future.

Do not rely on optimistically avoiding the subject or someone taking the first step and telling you (Dom told me he would ask for help if he needed it). However hard it is to bring up the subject and learn about it, I absolutely guarantee it is not as hard as burying a loved one.

And finally, if you are feeling suicidal, please remember that these feelings pass and you can be helped. Please tell someone you trust because you are loved and wanted here in this beautiful world.

*

The festive season overshadows the coming month. We cannot bear to create a facsimile of Christmas past with all the childhood rituals hollowed out and so decide to remove ourselves. Greg is in Newquay working until Christmas Eve and we haven't been back. Now seems like as good a time as any. And anyway, my instincts are pulling me to the sea even though I know it will be painful. I need to find a way to pierce the numb denial that has shut me down and disconnected me from myself, my feelings and everyone else around me. I cannot associate any of this with being me.

My throat closes with a flood of memories as we walk through the departure gate. My muscles tighten and my heart skitters like a captured bird as a hot flush of adrenaline turns me into a walking furnace. Jan grips my hand to steady me. It's caught me totally unprepared that every step retraces the route that Dom and I last took together. I sit in his seat on the very same plane and breathe into my feelings, wrestling my mind into seeing the pain as love. Tears break through as I see the Cornish coast below.

It's been a gamble to return so soon and waves of distress flow over me as we approach the hotel. I don't know if I can stay. We agree to see how it goes and to change the plan if we need to. Knowing I have an escape route makes it just about bearable.

The warmth welcomes me as I bundle my case awkwardly through the brass-plated revolving door. A Christmas tree laden with tinsel, twinkling lights and glittering baubles dominates the foyer. We won't be escaping the festive season here but at least no one will be expecting anything of us.

It would have been so understandable if the staff had been reticent on our return but we are swept up on a wave of hugs, wet eyes and 'how lovely to see you's.

I can't stop gazing at Greg and have to resist stroking his cheek for fear of annoying him. We're taking our first tentative steps to redrawing the family map. We wrap up against the blustery wind for a stride on the beach. Our voices are carried away so no one speaks, heads down. I'm swinging between troughs of despair and white-hot anger that it has turned out this way. Every now and then, triggered by a shift in the light or the breath of the wind, I am calm and sense the closeness to Dom that being here brings.

Mostly it is deep tiredness that colours the days and restless dreams that fill the night. We are the youngest of only a few guests, all of whom must have a reason to be hiding away. I spend hours sunk into a sofa chosen so that I can look out across the waves, crochet in hand. I am surrounded by the bustle of the staff preparing for the mass arrival on the 24th. It's worked better than I expected; we can be alone but not feel too lonely or exposed here. I'm nowhere near the word happy but at least I am still standing.

Jan, Greg and I spend hours at a time in companionable silence. My mind roams over memories stored as carefully as the decorations each year. 'Which is better?' we used to ask. 'Christmas or looking forward to Christmas?' Both boys loved it all: baking, icing the Christmas cake, visitors and party games, going to the cinema for the latest *Harry Potter* or *Star War*s movie every Christmas Eve, the standing jokes about four candles/fork handles in my stocking and Greg drinking Santa's milk. Dom especially loved this time, bouncing up and down with glee as we decorated the tree. I still have the handmade cardboard stars, coming apart at the seams but now more precious than ever.

At first I cannot even look at the cottages without trembling and nausea rising but gradually I begin to soften into the place, allowing it to work its magic. The weather is different from last time and the stormy seas add layers to my memories – hinting at the impermanence of everything. I now know, in the harshest way possible, that nothing can be taken for granted when it can be snatched away in a heartbeat.

Each day we retrace our steps around the coastal path and talk and talk or lapse into silence. I'm not able to even approach the sea for the first couple of days but I already know in my heart that I will need to face into this before I leave or I will go home with a sense of missing my connection.

The night before we are travelling home with Greg, we take him and all his mates out for pizzas. Once again, the sheer life force of youth is a tonic, and Jan and I soak it up gratefully. We've talked about how we want to handle Christmas and will decorate the tree together when we get home. Low key with occasional friend highlights – enough but not too much. Immie is joining us on Christmas Day and the many offers of sharing other family gatherings if we want to means we know that, somehow, looking after each other will get us through.

Pat to Kerry
Heading home for Christmas and setting our expectations VERY low. We saw the RNLI crew again and said proper thank yous to everyone. What a hell of a year. Thank God for good friends. See you soon. Love to all of you from all of us. xxxx

Kerry to Pat
Glad going back was a good thing. Will raise a glass to you all on Christmas Day. Let's get together soon. xxxx

In cold dawn light, Jan and I head out to say our goodbyes to whatever of Dom is here. I feel as if I am leaving part of me behind too. I can hear my teeth cracking under the pressure of my clenched jaw as I edge across the rocks towards the restless uninviting waves. We stand shivering, eyes on the far horizon. My heart pours out a stream of homeless love. The wind snatches up the silent messages and carries them away. We throw white roses into the deep. By retracing our steps, we may have found a starting point for the daunting road ahead. We will be patching ourselves together: the same trace elements of identity altered in an essential way. A change of state. However hard, I must face forwards. I know I will return and this gives me the strength to leave.

I cannot touch the water but I can keep my hand still on the tideline and wait until it kisses my fingers.

CHAPTER THIRTY-ONE

Kerry

Christmas Cheer

20 December 2017–1 January 2018

Saturday 23 December, 19.17
Hello Pat and Jan

Hope you're doing okay. I've been downloading my photos and found such a gorgeous one of you two, just had to send it through. Hope it doesn't do to you what looking at the photos of Cam pre-cancer does to me! Sent with good intentions and a reminder that good times will come again. Currently feel like a piece of honeycomb with wind whistling through my resilience…

Hope you manage Christmas okay – we'll be thinking of you. Sending so much love your way. Cannot wait to catch up with you in the New Year. xx

We meet with a clinical oncologist to discuss radiation treatment if the chemo hasn't worked. If it's needed, we'll have to get going on it quickly, as soon as he's had the final PET scan in mid-Jan, so the preparation has to start now. The session is entirely depressing – because of where the tumour is, in the middle of his chest, it's going to be difficult to avoid some damage to the lungs, and probably the heart too. For the boy who's desperate to get back to playing rugby, who's adamant that he will be fit enough for the school match against an Argentinian team in February, the last thing he wants to hear is that he might forever have reduced lung capacity. The oncologist warns us about the side effects, some that might surface in ten or twenty years' time, including secondary cancers. We drive home in silence. I turn the radio off. The last thing I'm in the mood for right now is Christmas carols.

The next day we're back at the Marsden again for chemo. It's the final one and I should feel relieved but the oncologist's words are still echoing in my ears. It feels as if we'll never be free. Some poor boy is throwing up behind a curtain in the teenagers' treatment room (where there are about eight chemo stations). I think it was designed so that there would be an opportunity for them to chat while they sit through the delivery but none of them ever makes eye contact. We try to ignore the vomiting – my heart bleeds for the poor parent sitting in there helplessly – but it's making Cam feel sick himself. We move into a side room. Cam sleeps and I just slump in the chair, catatonic, staring at his hair, which has started to grow back a bit, a baby fluff covering his skull. He's thrilled, though I'm worried it means the treatment has stopped working. The nurses bustle about, the whole ward is full of streamers and decorations – it's amazing the effort that they've gone to – but dark misery sits inside me like a stagnant pond. Hours later when the last bit of poison has been pumped into Cam, we head for home. He goes straight to bed, weak and sick.

*

For the next few days, we watch him struggle. He sleeps a lot, eats very little and Steve and I have whispered debates about whether we should go to Peterborough at all. Can we risk being away from the Marsden? But the idea of sitting gloomily watching Cam pick at his food on our own is way too depressing. By Christmas Eve, he's rallied a bit and we set off with Cam DJing in the front and me, Michaela and the dog squashed in the back. When we get there, it definitely feels like the right decision. Both Cameron and Michaela are happy to be with their cousins, who are a similar age, and it's a relief to all of us to be amidst noise, to have conversations that don't all revolve around blood counts, antibiotics, temperature taking, to talk about things outside the sphere of topics that have become our narrow focus. It's as though our world has withered. I rarely leave home except to go to the hospital, apart from walking the dog, which keeps me sane. Going out, even to town, which is about three miles away, makes me nervous unless we're all together. I can quite understand how people become agoraphobic. The woman I used to be, writing guidebooks, travelling around Australia on my own, boarding planes to the other side of the world as though I was getting on a bus to Nottingham, seems so far away now.

My sister-in-law has done a brilliant job of accommodating the extra four guests who'd dithered right up to the last minute, and is catering for ten instead of six. She's made loads of roast potatoes especially for Cam but he pushes them around his plate. I hate the idea of this being remembered as the Christmas our family sat there with long faces dragging everyone down with us. I make a determined effort to join in, complimenting the food and asking my nephew about his forthcoming mock A-levels. He's the same age as Cam and the contrast between his robust good health and Cam's pallor couldn't be more pronounced. Thankfully by Boxing Day, Cam is much brighter, well enough to have a beer. I force myself not to twitter on about not drinking too much, that his body won't be used to it. I need to get better at living in the moment but all I can see is the tick-tock of the clock towards

18 January when we will get the results of Cam's final scan and receive a pretty good indication of our fate. We all walk the dogs and when I stop my brain whirring for a moment, it could be any of the other Christmases we've shared with my brother and family. Except that the cold is making Cam's skin crawl and itch like mad where the hair follicles are coming back to life. We stop every now and again for me to rub his arms and legs. I have to force myself not to touch him for longer than required. I love that connection with him, the sense that I am helping in some way.

The day after Boxing Day, I call Pat on the way home. She's in the car with Greg and Jan and we keep our conversation brief and anodyne. Immediately afterwards a text arrives.

Pat to Kerry
Thanks for calling, Fish, I was a bit constrained in the car. Sorry I've been low profile, it's been all I can do to keep the fixed grin in place over the last couple of weeks. Having Greg home has been lovely but I'm already welling up at the idea of him going back to Cornwall. Even though I know it's absolutely the right thing. Would love to see you in the New Year. Am not back at work yet and God knows when I ever will be.

Kerry to Pat
No worries, Patti. I knew you had your family face on, which is why I didn't ask too many questions. You be as low profile as you want. I am here when you are ready to emerge. I completely sympathise with you not wanting Greg to leave. Who knew parenthood would be so intense? Xx

Monday 1 January

Kerry to Pat

Hi Patti. Hope you managed a decent evening yesterday. I imagine the start of a new year is an odd mixture of daunting and comforting. Very smug this morning as had my first sober New Year's Eve in years – Cam stayed out all night partying for the first time since he was ill and I was in emergency mode in case he fell flat on his face after half a shandy. And God knows whether any of his friends would have been sober enough to call an ambulance if it all went downhill! Had a good evening at our local Turkish – even did some dancing – though drew a line at belly-dancing. It goes without saying that I wish you both a peaceful and healing year this year (with plenty of drinking and laughing with us). Love you. Xx

Pat to Kerry

Hi Fish, We had a good night all things considered. Am impressed with you having no hangover! Hope Cam had a good night – well earned! For us it's like having an undertow of sadness that never goes away but we had good company. Feels mixed starting a new year but however hard, forwards is the only choice, isn't it? Counting our blessings as much as possible and off to Spain for a few days on Wednesday – can't wait to be anonymous and get a bit of sun! xx

CHAPTER THIRTY-TWO

Kerry

I Would Give Anything I Own

January 2018

The first two weeks of January see me in solitary confinement. I get the flu so badly, despite having had a flu jab for the first time ever, that I cannot get out of bed. I also dare not leave my bedroom in case I pass it on to Cam and he is too ill for his end of treatment scan on 17 January, which will tell us whether the cancer is still active. It's the only date on the whole calendar that I care about. Michaela and Steve take it in turns to poke toast and tea around the door, with me shouting at them not to come in. Days pass, then a week and I still can't do much more than stagger to the bathroom and back. The dog sits whining at the bottom of the stairs and after five days, I can't bear it any more. I spend the next week cuddled around her, her head on the pillow, with a certain air of smugness about her. And I am grateful for her company, her warmth and the comfort she brings as we count down the days to when we'll either be thrown a lifebelt of hope or weighed down with the lead of despair.

Steve suggests he could take Cam for his scan on the Wednesday but by some miracle, I am better by Tuesday. It's not that he couldn't do it but, just like the chemo sessions, I *have* to be there;

I cannot delegate. He's generous enough to let me do whatever Cam wants, whatever makes me feel better.

We head off to the hospital, on familiar territory now. As we wait to go into the scanning area, I stand with a daughter – about my age – and her mother – about my mum's age. They do that thing I've seen so many times. Their faces soften when they see Cam, thinking he's been so kind to accompany his mother, then descend into shock when they realise it's not me, it's him. The daughter is choked, desperately worried about her mother, and it's clear to me, again, that none of us is ever prepared for a goodbye. Regardless of whether the person is seventy or seventeen, we all want to hang on to our loved ones forever. I hope that's going to be possible. I hope I'll get to see my boy turn into a man. The older lady grabs my arm. 'Good luck. *Good luck.*'

Cam takes it all in his stride. He makes me laugh because he has his 'lucky pants' on – a grim, holey, hanging by a thread of elastic pair of underpants, the sort that I would previously have been ashamed for any doctor to clap eyes on and now I only care what gives him any sliver of comfort. After an hour of being pumped full of radioactive glucose, he makes his way, bum hanging out of the back of his gown, to the scanner that will determine his fate. I go in with him as he is fed in and out of the doughnut machine. Soon he is swallowed into it, just his Gucci trainers poking out. I know he'll love that picture so I quickly whip out my phone. I've no idea yet whether the photo will make me laugh or cry one day.

The next day we steel ourselves for the results. We've been lucky, just one night rather than a week of waiting. Cam drives himself as always. Steve comes with me. On the way there, Steve says, 'Do you remember going to that ball in Harrogate with Pat and Jan when they were fundraising for Candlelighters? [A Yorkshire-based charity that supports families with children facing cancer.] Do you remember the auctioneer talking about raising funds to help families "when their sky goes dark"?'

I remember it very clearly but I can't talk about it now when storm clouds are blocking out my own sky. But honestly, I can't believe the naivety of us back in 2003, bidding in the dinner-dance auction for a little electric car for Cam, shivering at the stories of tragedy and triumph we heard that night. We never imagined their stories would become our story, blundering on as we were in our belief that we were lucky, somehow immune. Today I can't understand what we thought made us so different but I guess we'd all be going to hell in a handcart if we went through life thinking it was only a matter of time before our kids got cancer.

We sit and I sweat, a ridiculous amount, as though my nervous system has blown a fuse. The oncologist puts us out of our misery immediately. There's no sign of cancer activity; Cam doesn't need radiation. Steve laughs. Cam and I cry. She puts the original PET scan side by side with the latest one on the screen. The radioactive glucose is attracted to the site of the cancer – and on the first one, it glows out like a big fat sunshine in the middle of his chest. In the new one, there's nothing. Cam sits WhatsApping his friends. I let it go. Steve and I listen to the upcoming regime of three-monthly scans for at least one year, four-monthly after that. For today, I allow myself to believe we'll get that far. We burble our thanks to the oncologist, to the clinical nurse specialist. But which words would actually be big enough, powerful enough to convey our gratitude? How could we thank anyone for giving us back our son? Our lives?

We let Michaela know, phone the grandparents, send a blanket text to our friends, then drive home in stunned silence. We take the obligatory photo of Cam – 'official remission day' – before he dashes straight back to school, job done. To Steve's astonishment, I go inside and cry until I think I might heave my heart up on a plate. I spend the rest of the day berating myself for not singing and dancing for joy, especially when Pat sends through a text: *Just heard the news. FANTASTIC xxxx*. What is wrong with me? This should be the best day of my life, but I feel as though everything holding me in and up has jellyfished to the floor and my feelings are lying there, a pulsating raw heap of emotion I no longer know how to manage.

When Cam gets home I rally, we drink champagne, he eats pâté, his favourite food, forbidden until now because of some danger to him that I never quite grasped. Cam doesn't miss a trick. He senses the era of us agreeing to anything might be drawing to a close and seizes the moment to get me to agree to a party at home the coming weekend. To avoid being the fun monitor, Steve and I go to the cinema. We come home to a house rocking off its foundations, a kitchen sticky with drink, the evidence of beer pong gluing our feet to the tiles. Cam is singing with his friends, arms around shoulders and there is joy. Energy pulses through the house, there's a sense of release, of relief. Some of the lads are smoking. I guess with the immortality of youth, they assume Cam has taken one for the team. Today is not the day. We walk into our sitting room just in time to see one of the girls throw up over my sofa.

I don't care. Yes, it's a low bar to be glad that Cam's still around for his friends to vomit on my furniture. But honestly, lucky me.

CHAPTER THIRTY-THREE

Kerry

The Elephant in the Room

28 January 2018

Pat to Kerry
Hi Fish, Hope you've stopped crying but I'm guessing relief is exhausting in a weird way. Any chance of a chat soon?

Kerry to Pat
Oh yes! I've stopped crying! Are you around?

Ten days after the clear scan I'm still trying to work out how to fill the days. I seem to have gone from a lot of activity to none, as though I've been sacked from a job that I never wanted but that gave rhythm and purpose to my life. I'm not yet mentally stable enough to go back to my 'real' job of writing and I'm ashamed of my feelings. I know there are so many parents at the Marsden who would love to be where I am. I feel guilty for not being happy, especially when I think about Pat and Jan facing into a whole new year that Dom won't be part of.

I haven't yet understood whether Pat can bear to hear about Cam or whether it's just really clumsy to even mention him. But I do want to speak to her to see how she's doing, so I ring, determined to be cheery because I am not the one that deserves the compassion. I don't realise we're going to have THE conversation today but when I hear her voice I know this is not something I can dodge, or do later by text. She makes it easy for me by asking how Cam is.

I plunge in. 'I've just got to come out with this and these might not be the right words but I feel awful talking about Cam when Dom's not here any more.'

She doesn't hesitate. 'I get that, Fish, but how would it possibly make me feel better if Cam had died?'

'I don't think it would make you feel *better* but up until now we were both in the same boat and now we're not and I just think it must be so hard for you to hear about other people's children.'

'Don't stop talking to me about Cam, otherwise our friendship won't be honest, it won't be real.'

The elephant leaves the room as we both sob down the phone. Eventually we default to our established coping mechanism of laughing in the worst possible circumstances and probably in the worst possible taste. Both of us agree that we're bloody glad we had no idea what life had in store for us when we met in 1984 at Freshers' Week. It's a stark contrast to us now, looking around the remains of our lives and wondering how to build from the ashes.

When I put the phone down, the same strength that under-pinned the conversation takes me back to the day of Dom's funeral when every time I looked over to Pat and Jan I couldn't believe they were still standing, still putting one foot in front of the other. Pat looked absolutely drained but I knew that whatever lay ahead, she would gather her resources to be strong for Greg. I've never known her quit at anything in her life and I am certain that even with the Herculean task of finding a way forwards, she's not going to start now.

CHAPTER THIRTY-FOUR

Pat

We're Getting There (Wherever There Is)

6 July 2018

'Do it for me. Do it for Dom. Do it for all of us.' As the final lines of my speech echo around the conference centre, applause erupts and then the whole audience of school teachers gets to its feet. I can see smiles of support and tears on many faces from where I am standing in the centre of the stage. I have not anticipated this and am struggling not to flee into the wings as I hold back the swell of sadness and relief that has engulfed me now that it's over. I've done it. I've practised day and night and have held myself together today by imagining Dom listening in. I never in a million years thought that this would be my life. Only nine months ago, my son was ripped away from me and I would never have believed at the time that I would be able to do something like this. It feels like a way of honouring him.

I'm finding it almost impossible to accept the first standing ovation I have ever received when it comes on the back of such terrible circumstances. I would give anything to be sitting in the audience right now watching Dom perform on the saxophone or singing the solo ballads he so loved.

On the way back to my seat I receive well wishes from everyone I pass but I'm so overwhelmed I cannot find words to reply and I'm fighting to contain my tears. Of all of these encounters, the one that sticks in my mind most firmly is the venue security guard in hi-vis who seeks me out and asks if he can shake my hand. 'Thank you so much for doing that. I'm a youth worker and I know it needs saying. You will have saved lives today.'

CHAPTER THIRTY-FIVE

Kerry

Looking Forwards and Letting Go

August 2018

In terms of pushy parenting, I've probably fallen into the category of 'Do try and get at least a B in English and Maths GCSE' with the odd bellow about 'Now's a good time to pull your bloody finger out' a fortnight before exams, but I hope I've never been in the out and out 'A* or die' variety of mothers. I've generally taken the view that my children are much more than their grades, while encouraging them to work hard enough to springboard onto the next stage of their lives.

However, when the day of Cam's A-level results arrives, I'm desperate for him to do well enough to get into his first choice of university. It's not that I think going somewhere else is the end of the world, but I would just love for him to get where he'd planned, for this bastard disease not to have changed the course of his life in any way. So in the lead-up to results day, I'm all 'Plenty of ways from A to B, darling', while secretly making a list of suitable courses in clearing and sending up promises of good behaviour if the universe could just grant me this small favour. It owes me.

On the morning, we've been told to be at school by eight if his place isn't confirmed on the UCAS website by then. We're just leaving home when the news comes in. He's got his place and has managed an A* in Business. I'm proud to an extent I'd hitherto thought was the reserve of tiger mothers. I have absolutely no shame in telling everyone who will listen how well he's done. And the same again the next week when Chaela, who has warned me that she'll be disappointed whatever she gets in her GCSEs, turns out not to be disappointed at all. I video her excitement and joy and even now play it to give me a lift. Sunshine on a screen and a credit to her resilience in an entirely shit year.

Two days before Cam is due to leave for university, there's a check-up scan, the third since he went into remission. He's had a cough that's lingered all summer. We've been back and forwards to the doctor's and don't quite believe that it's just a virus. Steve and I daren't fully embrace the idea of him heading off into a new life on Saturday in case, at the last minute, we have to say, 'Sorry, love, it's not going to happen for you.' So while I go through the motions of getting Cam ready for university, which is a pretty swift boyish process of 'I don't care what duvet cover I have/can you buy a corkscrew?', we're holding back on the conversations about what an amazing time he's going to have. But by Thursday afternoon, we get the news we were desperate to hear. The X-ray is clear.

Unusually, it's affected Steve much worse than me. 'I just couldn't tell him he couldn't go, couldn't face it.'

We have a huge flurry of activity getting him ready in a day and set off early Saturday morning. All my worries about whether anyone will look out for him, whether he'll ever tell anyone that he's been ill, whether anyone will notice if he goes downhill swirl around. I try not to nag about registering with the health centre but can't help it. I never quite manage to negotiate the fine line between getting him to agree to things so I don't have to lie awake worrying, and his normal eighteen-year-old desire to live, laugh and be like everyone else. As I drive, my body feels barely capable of holding in such a conflicting mixture of feelings – of course I'm delighted that he's moving on with his life, doing what he should be doing, but no one is going to be secretly inspecting him for 'return of cancer' signs like me and somehow, God knows how, I've got to learn to live with that.

Halfway to university, when there's still one hundred and seventeen miles to go, he taps me on the shoulder. 'Christ, this is a long way, Mum!' We laugh and I remind him how he thought Surrey University was far too close to home. He's never even seen a university. We didn't visit any because he was too ill, and struggling halfway across the country when there was no guarantee he'd get there seemed like a waste of scarce energy resources. I try to imagine him sitting in a campus room on his own, then swiftly try to unimagine it.

Mercifully, we've been allocated a measly half an hour of car parking to unload his stuff. I make his bed, put everything in his wardrobe and hug him goodbye. I force myself not to koala cling but it wouldn't take much. Of course I know he'll be a bit teary and lost for the time it takes us to drive to the motorway but he's on an exciting new path, the right one this time, where everyone won't be pointing him out as the cancer kid. The playing field has levelled slightly.

I recognise my own distress for what it is. Normal, not exceptional, heartbreak. Amen to that.

Reflecting on Our Experience of Grief

Pat

Grief for me was in the unimaginable, worst nightmare territory. The scale of taboos around the death of a child, plus the huge stigma and discrimination around death by suicide made it very difficult to find any guidance. In particular, Jan and I were completely on our own when it came to supporting Greg through his grief.

> **Pat**
>
> *'We really had no option but to create a DIY approach with a patchwork of beliefs, rapidly acquired knowledge, and previous experience of losing our parents. We threw everything we had ever learned at surviving the immense feelings that came with Dom's death.'*

Drugs and therapy

It goes without saying that we are all different here and speaking to the GP is a wise first step but we have learned not to judge others on their coping strategies (see further information about the British Association for Counselling and Psychotherapy at the back of the book).

> **Pat**
>
> *'On my doctor's advice, I took diazepam for the first few days after Dom died. I never would have considered it before but I was desperate – "unhinged with grief" was my*

reality, not just a loose term. Just because grief is expected doesn't mean it is possible to handle it alone.'

From a sceptical eyebrow-raising start, necessity converted us to experimenting with different therapies. Eye movement desensitisation and reprocessing (EMDR) has worked for both Kerry and me in handling the symptoms of shock. In the UK, along with other therapies such as hypnotism, it is not easy to find on the NHS, yet there is growing evidence that these approaches can work.

Pat

'One of the best things another suicide-bereaved parent said to me early on was "Work on the basis that you are in shock – that you will all be experiencing PTSD (post-traumatic stress disorder) – and find a qualified therapist who can help".'

In fact, all of our family members have had therapy of some sort to help us face what we are dealing with and although we have had to shop around to find approaches that suit our personalities, we have all found it useful to some degree.

Greg

I was nineteen when Dom died, in my second year of uni, comfortably in a pattern of surfing, drinking and studying. I never expected such a tragedy to happen at such a time when everything seemed easy, and when it did, the life I had been leading up to that point very suddenly disappeared.

The weeks and months that followed still remain mostly a blur to me, but I know this much: I fell heavily into a state of denial. As much as I refused to accept this at the time, the next five months of my life consisted of me alternately running and hiding from what had happened. I had friends visit me or I visited them; I went to Amsterdam, Portugal and Spain. But in between those wonderful moments of being able to forget, there were many more of me forcing myself to. If I wasn't smoking, I was out drinking with mates, although oftentimes both. My friends mainly let me get away with it given what had happened, but looking back, it's fairly clear why I'm not particularly able to remember much about that time.

Of course, this could never feasibly last. I had myself convinced even up until spring the next year that I was coping well with everything. Mum and Dad would always ask if I was okay, if I needed therapy or counselling, but I always just shrugged it off. I was fine – what would be achieved by talking about how absolutely unequivocally fine I was? It's easy to fool yourself into thinking like that, but had I been more honest with myself at the time, had I really looked at what I was doing to my own mental health, I probably could have avoided this next horrendous spell of my life.

At the end of March 2018, my parents and I had planned a week's escape to Ireland. It was my twentieth birthday just before we left, so of course I needed to have a proper celebration. This celebration just happened to turn into two of the most intense nights out I've had, the first one being a music event in Bristol that saw us not back in Newquay until 9 a.m., and after a quick nap, another night out leaving me awake until 6 a.m. – my flight to Ireland leaving at 8 a.m. Everything felt normal that morning – normal of course being immensely sleep deprived and hungover – until I boarded the plane. I sat in my seat, watching the cabin crew preparing for take-off, and suddenly I started feeling rather hot. I took off my jumper, and still felt as if I was boiling up. Then my heart started to pound faster than I'd ever known it to, and it was still increasing. The walls closed in, my throat along with them, I couldn't breathe, I needed to get out. This was my first ever panic attack, not that I knew it at the time. In one of the most humiliating moments of my life, just before the door was sealed, I begged the air hostess to let me off the plane, holding up my unfortunate co-passengers. Once back in the airport, I called Mum and Dad to let them know. They immediately said they'd come down, and I got my friend to pick me up in his van. During this whole period, everything just felt… odd. Like the world was no longer real. I had another panic attack in the traffic on the way home, and then tried to sleep it off until my parents arrived.

This feeling of unreality, near constant fear and regular panic attacks did not fade even slightly for another few months. I hated every moment of feeling like that, as if I'd never be normal again. I tried various different therapies, quit tobacco, weed and caffeine, ate better, meditated, anything I could think of to get myself back to normal. I'd never considered myself an anxious person, and here I was now feeling terrified nearly all the time.

Slowly, my derealisation (a feeling of disconnection from your surroundings) confined itself to my panic attacks, and while I was still anxious, it had transformed itself into intense health anxiety: any little symptom I either genuinely felt, or believed I did, I would research, and then diagnose myself with another life-threatening condition. This was easier to deal with than my previous anxiety, which seemingly had no cause. Over the next year, using a particular self-help method for anxiety, DARE, I learned to control and mostly cure my hypochondria. My panic attacks lessened and then stopped altogether (unless I found myself on a plane, and even then, I can now get through them).

I never truly understood my brother's anxiety until I developed my own form of it, and now I am more convinced than ever that mental health needs to be a priority in our modern world.

It is so important that people are aware of their mental health, and can find a way to talk about it – I very quickly realised that to try to battle through on my own would leave me far worse off in the end. Since my first panic attack, I've tried to be very open with my friends and family about my anxiety, and what I've seen among my friendship group is that my openness helped them to be more upfront about their own mental health too. When we chat about our mental health, it's often very casual and mixed in with other conversations over a pint, not a 'let's sit here and deeply examine your depression' sort of discussion. Personally, I've found this normalisation of mental health talk really liberating, and it helps me to see my anxiety for what it is: my brain overreacting to harmless stimuli in a misplaced effort to protect me. It makes it a lot easier to deal with as well, knowing that my mates will understand if I just mention 'I'm feeling really anxious' and get that I might be a bit quiet and out of it for a while – usually they start talking to me about unrelated stuff, and quickly my anxiety goes unnoticed. Had I kept it to myself, as I know it may seem less embarrassing to do, I'd be much, much worse off in that situation, getting inside my own head, focusing on the symptoms, and thereby increasing them. It's much easier for me to say, 'Oh dear, another heart attack. That's four this week!' than to stay quiet and try to ignore my heart palpitating at 180 bpm and the pains shooting down my arm. It might not be easy to open up at first – but trust me, it's worth it.

I've learned that grief will affect everyone differently, but there are certain things I believe will be detrimental to anybody going through it. It is easy to be drawn into the comfort of drugs or alcohol in those horrific times – but really, I don't recommend it, and don't let that be all that you do to cope. Be aware of your mental health – seek help after tragedy, even if you're not quite sure you need it. Deal with your loss in your own way, but do deal with it: running and hiding will not work forever.

At this point in time, two years after my brother's death, I still have anxiety, and I doubt I will ever be back to 'the person I was before'. But I am now more aware than ever of my emotions and anxieties, I have dealt with the death of my brother more effectively, and with that my life has moved forward into new and exciting times.

Pat

The physical impact of grief

In the way that no one talks about the real details of childbirth, no one told me how much grief affects you physically. I became a ninety-year-old lady, achy and stiff and for a long time my limbs would barely work. I'm so glad I was steered towards massage in the early days. It made me realise I needed to deal with physical symptoms up front rather than hope they would go away or I could just dose them with painkillers. It's hardest of all to do when I am sad or exhausted – the sofa is so tempting – but a gentle walk, some Pilates, sleep, a hot bath and a massage do make me feel better once I do them. I've also adopted the view that I am in recuperation, which has made me a bit more patient with how long it is taking me to get some of the symptoms under control. They still rise when I am under pressure, tired or when an event triggers buried memories.

Patience is a virtue

Realising that this will be a long road has helped us avoid 'waiting until we feel better'. We take the ups and downs as they come along but we try not to sit around poking our emotional wounds; when the feelings erupt, we deal with them with whatever resources we have. When we can laugh, we definitely do.

Acceptance

> ### *Pat*
> *'I was talking to a fellow passenger on a train comparing our experiences of tragedy in burying a son. He commented that he did not think he would ever get over it.'*

We went on to talk about this for the rest of the journey. It made me realise that my aim is to reach acceptance; not to move on but to take it with me. My experience of grief does not fit the neat linear pattern that Elisabeth Kübler-Ross's model suggests (denial, anger, bargaining, depression and acceptance). In fact I am surprised at how many counsellors still use it. I've been helped greatly by reading a book called *Grief is a Journey* by Dr Kenneth J. Doka, which proposes an approach of ongoing adjustment to the new reality. It reflects a more achievable process of getting used to carrying the weight of losing Dom and finding a new way to express my love for him. My personal experience so far is more like this:

My Grief + Mourning Map so far...

The black centre represents the early days when nothing else could get past the shadow of grief. Life still goes in and out of that space but there are also moments, days even, when it is less prominent. It now exists alongside other feelings; it's expanded my emotional range rather than replaced it but I know it will never go away.

Different cultures grieve differently

I've also found it useful to see things from a different point of view. In Aborigine culture, when someone dies, they are not mentioned by name or depicted in images. Knowing this allowed me to follow my strong instinct that I needed to let Dom go to find his ancestors. In Ireland there is a wake, a space to both mourn and celebrate a life lived. We used this to help us plan Dom's funeral gathering and it has helped me to focus my memories on happier times rather than stay stuck on the way Dom died.

Compassion from others has been welcome; a lifesaver. However, I have a sharp rejection of self-pity or victimhood because it makes me feel worse – powerless. I also have a defensive barrier to fend off comments such as 'You will never get over it.' Or 'It's the worst possible thing that could happen to you.' Thoughts like these destroy my hard-won hope. Wishing me strength is more useful than feeling sorry for me.

Pat

'When someone told me they had met many people bereaved by suicide and they could tell I would be one of those who found a way to carry on, I grabbed that drop of hope with both hands and carried it with me.'

In the early days Jan, Greg and I talked of how it could be the privilege of a wealthy society that expects all children to survive. In some places, children may not even be named until they reach their third birthday. All over the planet parents deal with the pain of losing a child every day. It does not mean that any of this loss is right – I would rather none of us had to suffer and it's a reflection of how far we have to go to create a truly fair world. It also would not have worked if someone else had tried to console us with these thoughts. While this wider perspective did not repair my broken heart, it did stop me asking 'Why me?' so often. It is a buffer against feeling sorry for myself, which sometimes works. I know it won't be everyone's way but this is my way.

Grief: the root of this word is the old French verb *grever*, which translates as 'to burden'. A burden that we, I, am learning to carry. It's the shadow-side of love. My relationship with Dom is different now – a love that lies within me. I live with him in my heart.

Kerry

While I hadn't expected to skip off into the sunset, I wasn't prepared for the after-shock of a reprieve after months of trauma and how other people thought I should react to a positive outcome.

> ### *Kerry*
> *'There was a certain sense that I was lucky – which of course I was – but my reaction to Cam's final clear scan was nothing like the elation people expected. Just weeks after he went into remission, people couldn't understand why I was still fragile, as though I should have moved on from it all by now. There was such a gulf between their view that he was "better" and my feeling that we'd cleared the first hurdle but still had five long years of scans before we could relax.'*

We mourned our previous certainty about the world. It was so shaken that the milestones we'd probably taken for granted before – the children finishing school, going to university, maybe getting married – no longer seemed something we could direct ourselves towards with any confidence.

Parenting versus gratitude

One of the big challenges in the aftermath of Cam's recovery was how hard it was to parent when I was so grateful for the fact that he was still here at all. Inevitably, any rules around mobile phones, going out, schoolwork and so on slipped when he was ill because it seemed ridiculous to make a song and dance about phones at the table when there were much greater things to worry about. There's also the natural tension between my desire to keep Cam safe now – obsessing about him eating well, not drinking too much, getting plenty of sleep – and his determination to make up for lost time. I'm painfully aware of how fragile life is, whereas Cam still demonstrates that teenage belief in his own immortality. It's a constant battle not to stop him living to keep him alive – and not destroying any sense of fun in our relationship by becoming a miserable old nagbag always banging on about vitamins. And then there's the whole shame around getting irritated about trivial things – trainers in the hallway, mud trailed through the house, being woken up at 3 a.m. – when I feel that I should never experience a second of annoyance again because I should thank my lucky stars he's still here. Very difficult to sustain!

Kerry

'It's a difficult balance to strike when you're parenting through a filter of "Do I care about this if he relapses in six months?" versus the hope that you're putting a decent human being into the world, with a sense of right and wrong that will serve them well at fifty and beyond. Being grateful that he's still alive gets in the way of thinking about what's right for the family now.*'*

Existing in the same but changed world

One of the hardest parts in the immediate aftermath of Cam's recovery was how to be 'normal' again. I recognised my behaviour as bizarre but didn't know what to do about it. For months after Cam went into remission, I wanted to talk about his illness, to everyone, to the extent of going into the butcher's and deliberately asking about whether I could order organic meat so I could lead into a conversation about Cam being ill and the necessity of him eating well. It was almost as though my brain was stuck on that one thing, so raw and so near the surface, that I couldn't hold it in.

Pat kindly explained that humans make sense of the world by telling stories and they tell them over and over again until they have processed their experiences. Over time, I feel less need to talk about him being ill, but even now, two years later, it doesn't take much to flip open the lid on that particular Pandora's box. Cam barely mentions it at all and Steve prefers not to on the grounds that he wants to think about happy things.

I was hugely encouraged by a woman who was kind enough to share her experience at a Marsden day for parents whose children had had successful treatment. She said seven years on, she no longer thought very much about her daughter's illness and didn't feel it defined her, or that it was even necessary to tell new people who didn't know her back then. I'm hopeful that I will reach that stage one day.

Grieving for the carefree future

I could have picked anything to rage about but the fact that Cam couldn't take the summer after his A-levels for granted, or even the one after that, seemed like such a huge injustice. I was filled with a fury I couldn't explain that this time of his life – the short interlude between leaving school and taking on the responsibility of work, mortgages and family – would be characterised by three-monthly scans to find out whether cancer would derail his life again. At his age, I'd never thought about my own mortality and it caused me tremendous grief that he had to. I'm sure it was linked to my impotence to fix things for him. On the upside, now in his second year at university, he definitely couldn't be described as a boy carrying the worries of the world on his back…

Looking after yourself when you don't care about yourself

Almost every well-meaning friend told us to look after ourselves: 'There's a reason why adults put their oxygen masks on before helping children on planes.' We found this practically impossible in times of crisis – what mother is going to put herself first when her child's life is under threat? Frankly, neither of us cared what happened to us as long as Cam and Dom made it through.

Self-punishment and almost deliberate sabotage of opportunities to relax happened to both of us: a superstitious belief that if we stopped being worried for one single second something would go wrong, that we alone were holding up the entire universe geared around keeping our children safe from harm. The truth is it's often only the professionals who can actually do anything.

Over time, however, we have had to learn to make space for ourselves otherwise the stable base wobbles and everything wobbles with it.

Here's a list of things that have helped or brought us comfort.

Nature's nurture

Walking our dogs. Picking out a few weeds but resisting the temptation to set ourselves a huge goal of clearing the whole flowerbed. Smelling the sweet peas, noticing the sky, filling the bird feeder, listening to the chatter of starlings, sitting in a hospital garden, eyes closed and feeling the warmth of the sun, breathing in the wet ground after rain. Somehow, all of these things helped us to remember the good in the world. They put our lives into perspective and helped us to accept how small we are and how big and ever-changing the natural world is. Just by taking the time to notice what was around us, we refilled the emotional tank just enough to stop us shouting at everyone who came near us.

Food

Although there were many days when putting beans on toast on the table was beyond us, never mind chopping a carrot, we both found it useful to focus on the discipline of making a meal. It was something practical we could do to bring the family together and stopped us going completely stir-crazy when we were at home in a full-time carer role.

Pat

'I had taught Dom to cook from very young, baking butterfly buns and white chocolate cookies. He came to love it and we often connected over experimenting with new recipes and sharing of the end result (his personal scone recipe is included at the end of the book for you to enjoy). When he was ill, Dom found great solace in choosing new recipes for us to cook together. I have a beautiful memory of us shelling broad beans shoulder to shoulder in companionable silence.'

Kerry

'At a time when the chemo had destroyed Cam's sense of taste and affected his appetite, cooking meals he fancied felt like one of the few things I could do to contribute to making his life better. I took a quiet satisfaction in sneaking cancer-combating foods such as broccoli and Brussels into sauces and curries.'

Cleaning

Pent-up nervous energy was burnt off on massive house cleaning binges: tidy drawers, sparkling windows, cobwebs banished, cushions thumped to within an inch of their lives. These are controllable tasks with visible results and they probably save a fortune in therapy too.

Kerry
'In a world that felt completely out of control, there was something very reassuring about creating order in a tiny corner of my home.'

Writing
All the things you cannot say, out of your head, and then put away.

Music
Matching a mood or changing it, music taps directly into all the emotions. It is a very personal thing that, in our experience, also comes with a big hazard warning because it has the ability to catch us off guard in the most inconvenient of places. Jan and Pat have both had times when they have had to dash away from a restaurant when something comes on that Dom used to sing.

Kerry
'I couldn't listen to the radio at all when Cam was first ill – every song seemed to be about love and loss and I had enough of my own to contend with. Conversely, when I did want to release some of the sadness and have a good cry, I played Bread's "Everything I Own" on repeat.'

Exercise
Whether it is walking, yoga, Zumba, squash, football, swimming or a workout, exercise has been the thing that we have had to force ourselves to do but has paid back in spades.

Trauma and stress are stored in your body and we've compared symptoms like a pair of hypochondriacs: tense jaw, stiff neck, swollen joints, sleeplessness, headaches, muscles painful with tension and legs so heavy that we have had trouble climbing the stairs, to name but a delightful few. Burning off some of the adrenaline and getting physically tired really has helped, even though neither of us was in the habit of regularly darkening the door of a gym.

Pat

'One of the things that stopped me even joining the gym was the thought that I'd have to explain what had happened to Dom. When I finally plucked up courage, I blurted out, "There's something I need to tell you really quickly." It worked and the trainer made me feel great about the fact that I was there at all.'

Whatever gets you through

If it works for you, is legal and does no one else any harm, why are you even hesitating to let yourself do it?

When life knocks you for six, one of the things you come out the other side with is a much longer list of things that help you when you really need it (scraping the bottom of the barrel of blessings again).

Pat's emergency top ten

- Listening to The Who at full blast.
- Reading poetry (I could not manage a novel), especially Seamus Heaney and Mary Oliver.
- Ranting in my journal.
- Forcing myself to contact a friend who lets me swear and makes me laugh.
- Getting outside in nature.

- Stopping resisting: when you need to, just go to bed and say to yourself 'It will feel better in the morning.'
- Doing a gym workout (never thought this would be me).
- Retreating to the sofa and watching crap TV or doing crochet.
- Having dinner and chatting with Jan. (We developed a secret codeword for when we needed to get off a topic before the emotions overwhelmed us. It was like learning a new language together.)
- Sending an emergency friends' WhatsApp call out for a rally round.

Kerry's emergency top ten

- Clearing out cupboards and getting rid of things. Going to the dump seemed to soothe me. Choosing a room and giving it a really good spring clean.
- Planting lots of bulbs.
- Walking with friends who let me say anything I wanted to.
- Meeting and talking to author friends so even though I wasn't writing, I still felt connected to my working world.
- Making and freezing soup for the days when I wasn't up to cooking.
- Walking the dog for miles and miles.
- Inviting people for dinner to distract us.
- Doing a Pilates class. Stress seemed to make all my joints very stiff. I hated going but I always felt better afterwards.
- Having a pedicure. It felt frivolous but having nice feet and giving myself permission to relax really gave me a lift.
- Having Michaela dye my hair. I couldn't face the hairdresser. I couldn't get beyond the 'Have you done anything nice this week?' and my inevitable blurting out of 'Sat in chemo for six hours with my son.'

Pat

'Here are some more positive postcards to stick around the house.'

> The sun's still shining behind the cloud.
>
> I might be broken but I am still breathing.
>
> The darkest hour is just before dawn.

Triggers and coping strategies

There are days you expect to be hard, especially anniversaries and birthdays, as well as Mother's/Father's Day, which even in good times rarely live up to the jolly photos on Facebook. But what about the unexpected triggers, the ones when you haven't already adopted the brace position?

Pat

The triggers are always changing. I cannot hear 'Titanium' without tears welling. The sight of scones in a bakery brings me straight back to the kitchen worktop with Dom in my apron. The change of the seasons brings with it a host of complex feelings. When I catch the light at a certain angle through the trees after the summer equinox, my heart turns towards those last weeks with Dom. I've tried my best to work with the grain of these memory keys: I use them as much as possible to find images of happy times with Dom.

It's harder to absorb and soften the most devastating moments that are triggered but I've found that by facing into them and reducing my instinct to resist, breathing into the sensations, I am learning. Sometimes I feel as if I am living in a metaphorical rip tide of devastation. It takes a great effort of will to keep swimming, to avoid being swept away, and there are also days when I do not have the energy so I retreat until it passes.

Pat

'I was once caught out completely when helicopters were buzzing overhead. I hid under a tree, folded over, fully back in the despair, claustrophobia and fear of the search for Dom. It was absolutely exhausting to deal with and released an avalanche of things I had forgotten about that time. My therapist was great: he suggested loud music, distraction or getting out of town. It was a relief to know I didn't have to battle on.'

Events linked to milestones that Dom will miss leave me feeling robbed. A-level results day, going off to university and even catching the start or end of the school day and watching other youngsters navigate their teenage years all seem to shine a spotlight on the things that we, he, will never have the opportunity to do.

Pat

'Initially when I sat in traffic watching groups of seventeen-year-old boys walk past, I'd see them in a completely different light – scanning for the pinched faces, the sad and unhappy ones. The feeling to protect was so strong I had to resist the temptation to wind down the car window and ask them if they were okay.'

Films, television and photographs all contain hidden pitfalls. Even *Paddington 2* triggered an unforeseen response because of the near-drowning scene. I have never liked violence in films and I now flinch or walk out of the room. There is no escapist pleasure in anything but the most anodyne of plots for me because real life has hurt too much.

Photographs on the phone are a mixed blessing. I have saved precious photos on the cloud, a hard drive and on my phone for good measure so that I know I will always be able to see Dom's face. But when a montage of our last summer holiday first pinged up on the iPhone after he died it was unbearable to watch. Now I treasure these collections although I control when I look at them.

Pat

'For me, it's not that time heals but that time passing has changed my perspective. I don't always succeed but sometimes I do manage to reframe my response into something more positive. At first any water was so triggering of Dom's death that I couldn't bear to touch it. Now I usually welcome it as a way of connecting with him.'

Jan

This is Pat and Kerry's book, and I'm in awe of both of them for writing it. It hugely resonates with me as though the events were from a few moments ago. To me, it feels sometimes as if we've been hurtling through space at the speed of light for just a few days only to return to earth to find that, for those around us, over two years have passed and people have moved on.

What has kept me anchored is my love for Patti and Greg, and the kindnesses of friends, family and acquaintances who have made the effort. In addition, a compassionate and highly competent therapist has helped me to focus on 'the life lived, not the life lost'. While triggers for difficult and sad thoughts will continue to arise, it is possible to avoid the two extremes of suppression and over-dominance, recognising my right to control some of this.

I'm then able to contain these extreme feelings by setting aside time for thinking about Dom. This process also assists me with unhelpful thoughts creeping in at other times. There is a Chinese proverb that goes: 'Expression of feelings leads to momentary pain and long-term relief; suppression leads to momentary relief and long-term pain.'

Kerry

Cam had been in remission for seven months but the week leading up to the year anniversary of his diagnosis in August was really difficult.

The follow-up scans every three months took on a pattern of relief for six weeks after a clear one, with a gradual increase in worry over the next month and a half. By the time we reached two weeks before a check up, life felt like a tinderbox of worry just waiting for a careless match.

> ### *Kerry*
> *'One of the most disappointing things is that my reaction to a clear scan is never one of unadulterated elation like you see in films. I feel completely exhausted and start snapping at everyone for leaving their dirty plates on the side instead of loading the dishwasher. It's almost as though now the big thing has receded for the next few months, my brain looks for ways to express anger that we've had to go through this.'*

We cope by working on a 'if there are three months between scans, we'll only let ourselves worry in the third month' rule.

Cam having a cough engenders a Pavlovian response in us because that's how the cancer started. With any illness, even something that looks entirely unrelated, we have to work very hard not to spiral off down the route of 'Could this be the cancer coming back?' Steve and I take it in turns to remind each other of the facts: that the last scan was clear, that he is a good weight, has a healthy appetite and looks well. We push back the irrational reaction of our fearful hearts with the rational thinking of our heads.

All photos, all events, fall into before and after August 2017. I don't know whether they always will but sometimes when I look at the photo collage in my kitchen of us all in Australia in 2015, I feel such a pain of longing for that ignorant bliss that I have to work hard not to fall into a vat of illogical self-loathing that I didn't anticipate what was over the horizon.

Cam being ill led to hyper-awareness of my own health. In the six months following remission, I was checked for bowel, ovarian and breast cancer. I think it's just something you have to go through because you are no longer able to say to yourself, *It won't happen to me.* It wasn't just self-indulgence – I also had a real sense of *having* to stay well to make sure I was around to look after Cam if he relapsed and to help Chaela navigate the consequences of living through such a trauma when she was just fifteen.

Unexpected reminders of how ill Cam has been at such a young age can trigger an extreme reaction. The day we received a letter to go to the clinic for a fertility check (so we could keep the NHS funding for sperm storage) – something I thought we wouldn't have to deal with until much much later when *he* was ready to find out – absolutely floored me. It made me feel that he'd never quite be living on the same level playing field as other boys his age. I dealt with it by allowing myself to feel devastated for a day, then I forced it into the 'It's not the end of the world; we're lucky he's still here' corner of my heart.

Saying out loud, 'My son is in remission from lymphoma' makes it all seem very real again, especially when I haven't prepared for it, such as the dentist's casual 'Any changes to your medical history?'

Thinking that I should be able to talk about it dispassionately in a medical way sometimes trips me up. I started telling my story to a woman at the gym who was static cycling to raise money for Bloodwise (a blood cancer charity). Her reaction – one of real kindness – made me burst into tears and ended in an unseemly debacle of her having to stop her fundraising cycle to smooth me out again.

Kerry

'Other people's reactions sometimes tip me over the edge. When I was making an appointment for us all to have flu jabs, the receptionist was querying why we needed them. When I said Cam had had cancer, she looked at his birth date, blurted out, 'Oh my God, he's only eighteen' and got all tearful, which had a domino effect on me.'

I have to work very hard not to ask, 'Are you alright?' in a panicky voice every time Cam rings me from university. There's always a little knot of anxiety that he's phoning to tell me he's feeling ill again.

A LETTER FROM KERRY

Dear Reader,

As a novelist, I've been in the privileged position of receiving letters from readers who've shared their own secrets and stories with me, saying they found elements of their real lives reflected in my fiction. However, it's the first time that I've written something so personal and it feels both liberating and terrifying.

There are so many reasons I wanted to write this book. Pat and I talk often about the fact that we've had to do the bit of motherhood that all of us hope to avoid – parenting at the furthest frontier with children who have life-threatening illnesses. The unpredictability of the outcomes for our sons made it hard to be us, but also hard to be around us. Friends, family – they all wanted to help – but what could they do or say that could ease the unrelenting misery of it all? I hope this book has shed a bit of light on that.

I also wanted to quash the myth that having a seriously ill child somehow turns you into a perfect parent. I did my best but I've yet to find anyone who is dramatically improved by being under fifty thousand times more stress than normal. I hope our stories will help anyone facing a traumatic situation to accept that catastrophic events stir up a lot of emotion, often feelings that are hard for other people to understand, or even to listen to in the first place. But that doesn't make you wrong or weak.

In these troubled times when the newspapers are full of everything that's bad in the world, it would be easy to get sucked into thinking there's no kindness left. I found the opposite – often from strangers or people I didn't know very well. In researching this book, I read back through my emails and found a lovely one from an author friend whom I've only met once or twice. '*Just wanted to say I'm thinking of you. Please don't feel you have to reply. I'm not expecting you to. Can't imagine what you're all going through, but will be lighting a candle for your lovely boy every day in church, and one for you too.*' I'm not religious but that touched me so much. I discovered the generosity of people who aren't bound by duty or obligation but just have a knack of making you feel a tiny bit better.

Which is why this book is also a celebration of friendship. Pat and I leant on each other so much in those dark days. I knew plenty of people whose parents had cancer, a few who'd had it themselves, but no one who'd had a child who might die. I didn't want someone to tell me he'd be fine – the oncologist with all the medical facts at her fingertips couldn't tell us that – I needed someone to be able to tolerate listening to the rational and irrational thoughts that come from knowing that keeping your child alive is out of your control.

In particular, when Cam was first ill, I needed to say out loud I thought he might die. Understandably, there wasn't a huge rush to be on the receiving end of that conversation. Pat could bear to listen without running for the hills. She didn't tell me that I mustn't talk like that or that I should manage my worries in a way she could bear to hear. She accepted that allowing me to voice my worst fears was a release in itself. It is a humbling testament to her generosity of spirit that despite her loss of Dom, she has never made it awkward for me to talk about Cam. She was among the first to congratulate me on A-level results day when he got into university despite his terrible final year at school. That requires a special strength and a very big heart.

I talked to Steve and he was a huge support to me, but sometimes we had so much of our own grief to manage, we didn't have the resources for each other's so I remain massively grateful to all the friends who did listen and, of course, to Pat, without whom this would have been a much lonelier journey. I hope this book will help anyone who's had a devastating diagnosis for a child – or any loved one – feel a little less isolated. Our world stopped when Cam was diagnosed but everyone else's lives, of course, kept moving forward and as time went on, I felt as though I was floating further and further from the shore of my old life.

In places, it probably sounds as though I'm having a pop at the NHS. There were inevitably times when we were frustrated because the world wasn't running to our urgent drumbeat of diagnosis and treatment. Overall though, I am beyond grateful for the brilliant care Cam received, especially at the Royal Marsden in Sutton, and so thankful that we live in a country where – in the main – cancer treatment doesn't depend on ability to pay. Pat's experience of mental health care provision was entirely different and if anything good can come from her story, I hope it will contribute to a change in that aspect of our NHS.

Finally, it would be disingenuous to pretend that when Cam went into remission, we all drifted back to our 'normal' lives. The following year, while we waited to see whether the cancer would return, was as challenging as when he was ill. An eighteen-year-old who's stared down the barrel of his own mortality, a sixteen-year-old sister who feels bottom of everyone's priority list and two parents glancing around the smoking remains of everything they used to take for granted do not make for a walk in the park. I say this in case anyone reading has recently had a 'trauma reprieve' and can't understand why they still feel terrible. My unscientific view is that when the trauma's happening, you're surviving, and afterwards you're processing the magnitude of what's happened. Grief and acceptance of trauma aren't linear and I still have days, two years on, when fear and sadness knock me off my feet.

However, in all of this, the one thing Pat and I clutch onto is that our natural optimism and belief that the world holds a good future for us has resurfaced. It's a huge tribute to her that she puts so much energy into helping other people facing similar situations. Writing this book with her has been a privilege and a blessing – we needed to trust each other absolutely to risk sharing the intimate detail of our lives before we could even consider allowing any of it to come under the scrutiny of the wider world. (See acknowledgements for Cameron's view on this.)

Thank you very much for not crossing the metaphorical street and being brave enough to read about experiences I hope will never touch you and yours. Now go and hug your children, especially those tricky teenagers, and tell them you love them.

With love to you and yours,
Kerry

A LETTER FROM PAT

Dear Reader,

Thank you for being brave enough to read this book. Having lost my beloved son, Dom, to suicide – death from a mental illness as I prefer to call it – I know all too well that I have come to represent one of the things that people find unimaginable in its horror. And understandably, it makes my story hard to read. As I have been writing this book, I have imagined it helping others feel less alone when their journey veers from the well-lit main roads.

In the aftermath of Dom's death, I came to see with absolute clarity that the stigma and lack of understanding about mental health in our society contributed to him feeling so alone and unable to ask for help. It was also a factor in me not knowing how to help more effectively – to spot the signs. We as a family have paid the highest price: an empty place where Dom should be and never-ending 'what ifs' to live with.

To have gone through this without the love and support of our friends, family and community would have been a much tougher experience. I would never wish misfortune on anyone but having Kerry living through Cameron's cancer treatment at the same time as Dom was ill meant that our friendship was a lifeline. Another mother who knew that I was imperfect but did not deserve this, that Dom did not deserve this, and who I could share my darkest fears and frustrations with. We talk about the 'three o'clock in the morning friends' and now I know just how important they are.

In all but the very darkest of days, Kerry and I still managed to find some bleak humour in our texts, calls and emails. We started to put our stories together on many a dog walk as a way for both of us to make sense of what life had thrown at us. As we did so, it became clear that there was a lot that we had in common but also a massive gulf between the treatment of Cameron and Dom. In particular, there was a vast difference in the way Steve and Kerry were directly involved in Cameron's treatment decisions when Jan and I were struggling even to be kept up to date.

Gradually, as part of surviving our loss and to scrape the barrel for something good to come out of this, I decided to do all that I could to help others avoid the pain and grief-loss that we live with every day. So, I started to talk and write about our experience to raise awareness and understanding of mental health, and especially suicide prevention for young people. We lose more than 250 school-age children a year to suicide in the UK alone and it needs addressing urgently. It's a tragedy that most of us feel will never happen to us, but it does and the impact is massive and wide-reaching.

Working with Kerry on this book has become an extension of that desire to help and having her by my side has made it possible to do. It's been a privilege to learn alongside such a generous, skilled and sensitive author. I have written as if telling my story to caring friends – something I did often in the early days to come to terms with what had happened. It is my, Jan and Greg's hope that in sharing such a private part of our family life we can do our bit for bringing mental health care into the open. I also want to honour Dom, who tried so hard to overcome his mental health problems. We will love and miss him forever. He is in our hearts.

This book is also a tribute to friendship – not just Kerry's but to all my dear friends (including those who come under the category of relation as well) and to love, without which I would not have had the strength to make a cup of tea, let alone write a book.

It probably won't be the easiest read but it is intended to be optimistic and I hope that it is useful. If it starts one conversation, or saves one life, then it will be worth it.

Take good care of each other and be kind to yourselves,
Pat

SURVIVAL KIT SUGGESTIONS

Note from Kerry: I am quite embarrassed by the enormous list of resources Pat has used to help herself. I'm sorry to have very little to contribute here apart from *Grief Works* by Julia Samuel, which made me feel so much better about my reluctance to stray very far from home, explaining that people who've experienced trauma sometimes feel the need to stay within an environment they deem safe when everything else seems so out of control. My most effective way of helping myself, apart from counselling, was talking about what had happened ad nauseam, to just about anyone who would listen. I now recognise this might not have made me the top dinner party guest in the last couple of years… Writing this book has also helped me process and archive a lot of my most unhelpful thoughts. However, I do feel that a lot of Pat's resources are relevant to anyone who has suffered a severe trauma, even if they don't relate directly to childhood cancer. Steve coped in an entirely different way from me (see below) – I think it's fair to say he was a lot less of a drain on his friends!

Steve

For me, one of the hardest things about Cam's illness was dealing with the uncertainty about the future. I've always been interested in how different cultures/eras of history deal with adversity and a friend recommended looking at Stoicism. I liked what I read and tried to adopt some of its practices. At its heart is a system based on action, rather than endless debate. It focuses on what we can control, not on what we can't. At its core is the idea that we can only control ourselves and our character, which allows us to be steadfast and strong, even in the toughest of times. One of my favourite readings was the *Meditations* – written by Marcus Aurelius, Roman Emperor and Stoic. This particular reflection really spoke to me during Cameron's illness:

> *If you suffer distress because of some external cause, it is not the thing itself that troubles you but your judgement about it, and it is within your power to cancel that judgement at any moment. But if what distresses you is something that lies in your own disposition, who is to prevent you from correcting your way of thinking?* – *Meditations 8.47*

Books, websites and other resources – Pat

Thich Nhat Hanh – *Peace Is Every Step.* I am so grateful that I had read this book long before we lost Dom and turned straight back to it when we returned from Cornwall.

Thich Nhat Hanh – *Reconciliation: Healing the Inner Child.* I read this about a year after Dom died. It helped me notch forward when I'd got stuck. The Buddhist outlook won't suit everyone but it works for me and frankly, as long as it's not hurting anyone else, that's all that matters.

Matt Haig – *Reasons to Stay Alive.* I found this book hard to read because I kept wishing Dom had found it or that it could be injected in at the age of, say, fourteen as a vaccination against suicidal crisis.

Jenni Murray – *That's My Boy.* I leapt on this book when the boys were little and then went back to it when I needed someone wise. Also, knowing that she has battled with her own breast cancer and grief gave me both hope that I might be able to return to work and the permission to try.

Dr Peter A. Levine – *In an Unspoken Voice*. I normally have a few fiction books on the go and a queue of 'ready to reads' on the bedside table. But when Dom died I could not read fiction, found no joy in sham scenarios when real life was far too full of drama and tragedy and violence. Many of the books still sit unread from that time – tainted by what stopped me reading. For a while, I read nothing and when I did start again, it was triggered by an urgent need to try to understand what might have been going on for Dom. The first things I read were the training files for Mental Health First Aid. Waves of sickness and prickly sweat rose as I recognised all the signs and symptoms I did not know about. This book did the same but it also transformed my world view. Dr Levine's work helped me understand how Dom had come to the point of collapse and how I needed to work with my physical trauma symptoms if I wanted to be free of them. This is the book that got me into the gym and into more trauma-based therapy.

Dr Edith Eger – *The Choice*. I became drawn to anyone who had had a harder life than me as part of resisting the 'worst thing that could ever happen to you' role along with its accompanying victim status. So when I came across this via the book reviews in the *Observer Magazine* I read on. The blurb hit me like a blast of arctic air: 'I had to choose between focusing on what I had lost or being grateful for what I still had.' I changed my screen saver from a picture of Dom to one of Greg that day and have tried to give Dom his 'fair share' of my headspace since then. Hearing a story of not only surviving such unimaginable horror but assimilating the experience, building a positive life and having compassion even for the perpetrators, was inspirational for me.

Stephen Grosz – *The Examined Life*. This helped me realise that I will never know for sure what was going on for Dom and that the type of therapeutic or psychiatric interventions we use are only the beginning of how mental health treatments will develop in the future.

Bessel van der Kolk – *The Body Keeps the Score*. This is an incredible book looking at trauma holistically. It's about as readable as the subject can possibly be and it's a great way to learn about so-called alternative therapies that might just be the next wave of mental health treatment improvements.

Dr Kenneth J. Doka – *Grief Is a Journey*. Jan's therapist put us on to this book and it has been our 'how to' manual for grief. We've passed it on to others and, so far, without fail they have found it helps them. I'd love it to be a must-read for grief counsellors. The section on suicide and siblings is more limited but the general grief theories are easy to grasp and made me feel less alone. I'm still dipping into it now.

Yann Martel – *Life of Pi*. I can still remember reading this looking over my favourite mountain in Ireland six months after my dad had died. I was really struggling with deep shock, staggering through work and barely functioning at home. When I read the line about facing grief rather than running away, it hit me at the right angle, slicing through the cognitive fog. From that day, I started to heal, turned to face the painful feelings. I've drawn on that experience to find my way through the heartbreak of Dom's death.

Anne Morrow Lindbergh – *Gift from the Sea*. This book is so gentle and softened my heart in just the right way.

Tove Jansson – *A Winter Book*. Reading this helped me connect with nature and also guided my instinct to retreat and restore when Dom first died.

Naja Marie Aidt – *When Death Takes Something From You Give It Back*. This one found me. For a long time, I could only read the title but I know it has gifts inside because I have read occasional pages. It is written by a mother whose son died in a tragic accident. It charts the first terrible year of grief and re-emergence as the shock wears off.

Seamus Heaney – *100 Poems*. The connections with Ireland link me back to my roots and these poems tip me into the universe of grief and then safely bring me back out again.

Mary Oliver – *New and Selected Poems, Volume One*. This book helped me notice nature. It fell open on a poem about a starfish and I was hooked.

Barry McDonagh – *Dare: The New Way to End Anxiety and Stop Panic Attacks*. This is the book that Greg found so useful.

Websites

www.gomadthinking.com – Our friend Andy Gilbert from Go M.A.D. Thinking trained both Jan and me in his thinking approach many years ago. It was Andy who sent us the email about goals that we pinned up around the house.

www.thubtenchodron.org – There is a beautiful prayer-like meditation on this website especially for those who have lost someone they love to suicide. It is the one I read every day for forty days and I still carry it with me now.

www.beyondblue.org.au – The Australians seem to be ahead of us on mental health and suicide. This website is one of those I wish I had found before Dom died rather than after. It might have saved his life.

www.refugeingrief.com – Megan Devine hosts this and it has come up with a lot of insight and personal experience that's helped me.

www.tcf.org.uk – This charity specifically supports bereaved parents and their families. There is lots of guidance about how to help and what to say.

www.cruse.org.uk – This charity supports those bereaved in any circumstances.

www.uksobs.org – This group specifically supports those bereaved by suicide.

Podcasts: Griefcast

TV: *When Calls the Heart, The Durrells, The Crown, The Thick of It* or basically any box set to your taste that distracts you or makes you cry when you need release.

Helpful websites and charities – Kerry

www.clicsargent.org.uk – Clic Sargent is extremely good at supporting families. The website has a wealth of information about everything from the financial side of cancer to dealing with the unpredictable emotions that come with a child's diagnosis. It also supports young people in continuing with their education throughout treatment as well as providing opportunities for them to connect with other people in a similar situation. A grant (at the time of writing, £170) is available for every child who registers to help with sudden expenses such as travel to hospital, parking, accommodation and so on. Cam never wanted to be involved and wouldn't register but for the right child, it could be a very useful support.

www.macmillan.org.uk – Macmillan offers information about specific cancers plus financial and practical support for caregivers. When Cam went into remission, I had some counselling at one of their local hubs.

www.teenagecancertrust.org – This charity supports young people aged between thirteen and twenty-four, funding twenty-eight specialist teenage cancer units within NHS hospitals. Its website offers specific sections of advice for parents, siblings and friends when a young person is diagnosed with cancer, as well as a 'Young Person's Guide to Cancer' that you can download from the website or email for a hard copy.

www.youngminds.org.uk – This charity focuses on young people's mental health. It has guides dealing with specific problems – anorexia, depression, obsessive compulsive disorder – with advice about where to get further help. Pat recommended this charity to me when we didn't know how to support Cam when he went into remission and was so angry about everything. It gave us guidance on finding counsellors in our area.

www.bacp.co.uk – British Association for Counselling and Psychotherapy. This is a good starting point for exploring the different therapies available and for finding an accredited therapist near you.

Let's talk about suicide – Pat

One of the very hardest things I have dealt with since Dom died is finding out that a lot is known about suicide prevention and NO ONE TOLD ME.

In an emergency call 999.

If you are worried about someone or have suicidal thoughts yourself, there is help out there and plenty of information. These are just some of the people you could contact:

- HOPELINEUK: call 0800 068 4141, text 07860 039 967, email pat@papyrus-uk.org (not the author). HOPELINEUK is run by Papyrus Prevention of Young Suicide, which not only offers support to people up to the age of thirty-five who are having suicidal thoughts, but also offers advice to parents, carers and professionals in supporting someone who is having suicidal thoughts.
- www.stayingsafe.net (for suicide safety planning).
- www.zerosuicidealliance.com (Suicide – Let's Talk online free training). This might be the hardest thing you ever watch, especially if you are worried about someone but I

absolutely guarantee that it is not as hard as losing someone and then finding out you might have been able to do something.

- Samaritans: call 116123, email jo@samaritans.org. The Samaritans are available on the phone, by email or letter and for anyone who needs to talk not only for suicidal crisis. Please note that if it is email it might not get seen straight away (up to 24 hours) so if it's urgent be brave and pick up the phone. If you don't know what to say just tell them that and they will pick it up from there.

DOM'S SCONES

Ingredients

- 500g/1lb 1oz strong plain flour, plus a little extra for rolling out
- 80g/3oz softened butter, plus a little extra to grease the baking tray
- 80g/3oz caster sugar
- 2 free-range eggs, room temperature
- 5 teaspoons baking powder
- 250ml/8½fl oz milk
- 1 free-range egg, beaten (for glazing)

Method

Preheat the oven to 220°C (200°C fan assisted)/425°F/Gas 7.

1. Lightly grease a baking tray with butter and line it with baking or silicone paper (not greaseproof).

2. Sieve flour (450g/15½oz) into a large bowl and add the butter. Rub the flour and butter together with your fingers to create a breadcrumb-like mixture. Hold the mixture high above the bowl as you crumble it to add air and do this for a good few minutes.

3. Add the sugar, eggs and baking powder and use a wooden spoon to turn the mixture gently. Make sure you mix all the way down to the bottom and incorporate all of the ingredients.

4. Now add half of the milk and keep turning the mixture gently with the spoon to combine. Then add the remaining milk a little at a time and bring everything together to form a very soft, wet dough. (You may not need to add all of the milk – if too wet, add more flour when working dough until it feels right.)

5. Sprinkle most of the remaining flour onto a clean work surface. Tip the soft dough out onto the work surface and sprinkle the rest of the flour on top. The mixture will be wet and sticky.

6. Use the palms of your hands to gently spread the dough. Fold the dough in half, then turn the dough 90 degrees and repeat. By folding and turning the mixture in this way (called 'chaffing'), you incorporate the last of the flour and add air. Do this a few times until you've formed a smooth dough. If the mixture becomes too sticky, use some extra flour to coat the mixture or your hands to make it more manageable. Be very careful not to overwork your dough.

7. Next, roll the dough out: sprinkle flour onto the work surface and the top of the dough, then use the palm of your hand to lightly press out from the middle until it's about 2.5cm/1in thick. Use the palm of your hands to press the edges back in if they get too thin.

8. Using a 6cm round plain pastry cutter, stamp out rounds from the pastry and place them onto the baking tray. They like to be cosy: it helps them to bake evenly. Dip the edge of the pastry cutter in flour to make it easier to cut out the scones without them sticking. Don't twist the cutter – just press firmly, then lift it up and push the dough out.

9. Once you've cut 4 or 5 rounds you can re-work and re-roll the dough to make it easier to cut out the remaining rounds. Any leftover dough can be worked and rolled again, but the resulting scones won't be as fluffy (Dom never took a second pressing!).

10. Place the scones on the baking tray and leave them to rest for a few minutes to let the baking powder work. Then use a pastry brush (or your finger if you don't have a brush) to glaze them with the beaten egg. Be careful to keep the glaze on the top of the scones (if it runs down the sides it will stop them rising evenly).

11. Bake the scones in the middle of the oven for 15 minutes, or until the scones are risen and golden-brown.

12. Leave the scones to cool a little, then split in half and serve to taste: Devon, Cornwall or Dom style.

To serve 'Dom style'
Rodda Clotted Cream (dollop & spread to edges). Duchy Organic Raspberry Jam on top. Mix jam a little into the cream with back of spoon. Leave lids off jam and cream next to crumbs, knife and spoon on worktop.

Secret top tips
Work dough by folding, only use for one batch (discard the leftover dough). Sieve the flour twice.

Best served under a soft blanket with an episode of
Modern Family or *Friends.*

KERRY'S ACKNOWLEDGEMENTS

Where to start with a book like this? So many people to thank. Top of the list is the histopathologist who realised that Cam didn't have Hodgkin's lymphoma but the rare Grey Zone, which required a different treatment. On Cam's birthday and at Christmas, I imagine him or her looking down a microscope and saying, 'I don't think that's quite right.' I've no idea who it was. They might not even know what a huge difference they made to us but if they are having a bad day at work, I hope they can hold the image in their mind of me hugging my boy when he gets home from university. To them, it might just be a job (though I doubt it). To me, it is the world.

Next on the list is our oncologist at the Royal Marsden and our Chief Nurse Specialist. I can't thank them both enough for their kindness, patience and expertise. Ever. And a huge cheer to all the staff at the Royal Marsden's Oak Centre for Children and Young People. How they do what they do with such grace and efficiency, I have no idea.

Thank you to my family for supporting me when they had their own grief to deal with – it's hard for grandparents because they were devastated not only for Cam but also for me. Thank you to the friends who took me out when I was properly poor company. I haven't mentioned by name everyone in this book who dug in and played a part in keeping us plodding forwards. I'm not going to pinpoint anyone now because I know I'll miss someone out but I had some great friends who supported me through this darkest of times. The people who cooked for me, walked with me, messaged me, wrote letters, were brave enough to ring for news and still invited us out long after we'd stopped being fun to be around. Those who came to the hospital to visit Cam in the early days. Everyone who still asks how he is. The teachers who took time to help Cam both during and after his illness, especially Dan Richards. (I do have to pick him out. Above and beyond the call of duty.)

My fiction editor at Bookouture, Jenny Geras, who so kindly took over the editing of my next book and released me from work stress to concentrate on Cam.

Clare Wallace, my agent, who believed in this book from the very beginning and was just brilliant when Cam was ill. I don't know how she does it but she always manages to say the right thing in every situation. Our editor, Claire Bord, whom we knew was the perfect fit for this book right from the first meeting and has been a wonderful champion at every stage of the way.

And to everyone who was brave enough to say, 'I'd like to read that' whenever I spoke about this project.

To Pat, for being someone I could trust with my raw vulnerability and the worst version of myself without fear. And also for working so hard alongside me to make this story a process that not only healed and helped us but that we hope will give other people some comfort too.

Finally, thank you, Cam, Michaela and Steve for allowing me to share our story with the world (and of course, for being your resilient, resourceful and funny selves). On that note, I'd just like to say that Cam has generously and willingly allowed me to talk about what happened to him: he hasn't read the whole book because I think it is too big a burden at his age to read at length about my despair but he has listened to extracts where I have recounted intimate details of his journey in order to help other people. In fact, although I'd dreaded reading it to him and sparking reminders of the worst time of his life, we actually laughed a lot looking back at what he'd gone through. Hats off to you, Cam, I am so proud of you.

Michaela was so young to have to deal with the knowledge that her parents couldn't fix everything and she did it with such courage and strength. It's only now with the distance of time that I understand how brilliant she was – and is.

I'm struggling to find the words to express my gratitude to Steve. Just knowing that he loves Cam as much as I do and would do anything at all to make it right was a huge comfort. It's a privilege to have had his hand to hold through the last three years when we had no idea what 'For better, for worse' might entail.

I consider myself very lucky.

PAT'S ACKNOWLEDGEMENTS

The heading does not seem to do justice to the incredible support that Jan, Greg and I have received from all sorts of people, often when least expected and most needed.

One of the many things that the last two years have taught me is that kindness and taking time to support someone are literally life-saving. When I was on my knees with despair, begging the world to stop turning just for a second so I could get my bearings, the people who noticed and came to give me a hand up have my everlasting gratitude.

First and foremost, thanks to Jan and Greg for trusting me to tell part of our family story and for supporting me when I was writing it and revisiting a lot of the feelings from that time. Thank you both for being my centre of gravity and of joy. I count my blessings for you both every day.

Thanks to Clare Wallace, the talented agent who took me under her wing as I started out on this book. Thank you for believing in it and for taking a gamble on me. It's a privilege to learn from you.

Thank you to the team at Bookouture who have seen the significance of this book right from day one and especially to Claire Bord, who has balanced absolute professionalism with personal warmth all along the way. Every now and then life connects me with people I feel I was meant to meet and here we are.

To our families, who continue to support each of us in so many ways while dealing with their own grief. Thank you too for keeping Dom in the conversation and in your hearts.

Thanks to our friends from both nearby and far and wide who have stuck by us; kept us sane; forgiven our forgetfulness; fed us; walked the dog rain or shine; learned how to look after us in territory none of us wanted to be in. We'll never be able to repay the debt mountain so we are paying it forwards. We count ourselves honoured to be your friends. I hope you will all understand when I say a special thank you to Emma, Jackie, Kate, Paul, Peter, Sarah, Soff and Jez. To those friends who for whatever reason have not been able to 'step in': no hard feelings. It is difficult for me to understand but I do know that sometimes we are not in the right space to be the one who helps and that is okay.

I want to thank the emergency services: the paramedics, police and coastguard, the NHS. I wish we were celebrating a happy ending. Mental health services need a massive dose of funding for research into new treatments and for more staff to look after those who are ill. That does not mean that individuals are not trying their very best to support those living with mental illness. I'm glad to be working with you to save lives.

To the Newquay RNLI crew, who risk their own lives to save others and who brought my boy to shore and shared our grief with such humble courage. Thank you for allowing us to become part of your community. You are in our hearts always.

To Gillian and Rachel, who first heard me talking of the book idea and fanned the flames with their enthusiasm. I hope it lives up to expectations, girls.

Thanks to the wonderful hotel teams who continue to welcome us with open arms. You have given us a home from home to return to. A place of peace.

Thanks to everyone who has raised funds in Dom's memory. Jan and I are so touched by your generosity.

Thanks to all my professional friends who have believed in me and cajoled me back into the world, opened doors for me and didn't take it personally if the time wasn't right to walk through them.

Love and thanks to Greg and Dom's friends who have been brave enough to spend time in the shadow of our grief – lighting up the dark moments with their thirst for life and laughter.

Thanks to Jo, my best friend from school, who I miss so much and who managed to tell me I was 'entering my creative phase' as a parting gift.

And last but definitely not least, thank you, Fish, for your friendship and for having such generosity of spirit in sharing your talent for writing (and agent and publisher) with me and for being patient as I've found my voice. It's been a deep journey to create this book. I wish we hadn't had to write it but I can't think of a better writing companion.

BOOKS BY KERRY FISHER

Printed in Great Britain
by Amazon